651.37
C18

Careers in Focus

CLERKS & ADMINISTRATIVE WORKERS

Ferguson
An imprint of ☑®Facts On File

Careers in Focus: Clerks & Administrative Workers

Copyright © 2004 by Ferguson

Ferguson
An imprint of Facts On File, Inc.
132 West 31st Street
New York NY 10001

Careers in focus. Clerks and administrative workers.
    p. cm.
Summary: Defines the top twenty-one careers in office work, discussing the nature
of the workk, educational or training requirements, getting started, advancement
possibilities, salary, employment outlook, and sources of more information.
Includes index.
    ISBN 0-8160-5484-3 (hc: alk. paper)
    1. Clerical occupations—Juvenile literature. [1. Clerical occupations. 2.
Vocational guidance.] I. Title: Clerks and administrative workers. II. Title: Clerks
and administrative workers. III. J.G. Ferguson Publishing Company.
    HF5547.5.C335 2003
    651.3'7'02373—dc22   2003013435

You can find Ferguson on the World Wide Web at http://www.fergpubco.com

Text design by David Strelecky

Printed in the United States of America

MP FOF 10 9 8 7 6 5 4 3 2 1

This book is printed on acid-free paper.

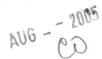

Table of Contents

Introduction

Clerks and administrative workers are employed in a wide variety of work environments, from grocery stores and collection agencies to corporate law firms and executive offices. Their duties vary from general bookkeeping, typing, and office tasks to more specialized positions such as medical transcription and insurance policy processing. Many different types of employers hire secretaries and administrative workers, and these employees have varied levels of responsibility depending on the size of the firm, business, or institution. There are 3.9 million secretaries and administrative assistants employed throughout the United States, as well as 5.1 million information and record clerks, making this field one of the country's largest. Approximately three out of five secretaries work for firms providing services in fields such as education, health, business, and law.

Secretarial or administrative assistant work is often entry level: Many employees use their experience in secretarial work as a stepping-stone to more advanced positions. However, a considerable number of workers stay within this field and some advance to positions of more responsibility, such as executive assistant or senior administrative assistant. After gaining experience, clerks in stores and hotels may advance to management positions.

Clerks and administrative workers must be able to interact with all different kinds of people, and they must be computer literate. These workers must also be organized, attentive, and able to follow directions. The secretary or receptionist is often the first person that a client sees, so a professional appearance and friendly demeanor are a must for workers in this field. Clerks and administrative workers should be detail-oriented and have patience to complete repetitive tasks.

In recent years, advances in technology have revolutionized traditional secretarial tasks such as typing or keeping records of correspondence. The use of email, scanners, and the Internet has had a major impact on this field and will continue to do so in years to come.

As a whole, clerks and administrative workers are expected to experience average employment growth over the next several years. However, several areas within this field have experienced growth in recent years, including medical transcriptionists, medical secretaries, and legal secretaries. *Occupational Outlook Quarterly* projects that medical transcriptionists will experience employment growth of approximately 30 percent from 2000 to 2010, which is faster than the national average for all occupations. As the population ages and grows, more medical services are required by the elderly, which has also increased the need for medical secretaries and medical transcriptionists. Legal secretaries have seen increased growth as the number of court cases rises each year.

Each article in *Careers in Focus: Clerks & Administrative Workers* discusses a particular education occupation in detail. The articles in this book in appear in Ferguson's *Encyclopedia of Careers and Vocational Guidance,* but they have been updated and revised with the latest information from the U.S. Department of Labor and other sources.

The **Quick Facts** section provides a brief summary of the career including recommended school subjects, personal skills, work environment, minimum educational requirements, salary ranges, certification or licensing requirements, and employment outlook. This section also provides acronyms and identification numbers for the following government classification indexes: the Dictionary of Occupational Titles (DOT), the Guide to Occupational Exploration (GOE), the National Occupational Classification (NOC) Index, and the Occupational Information Network (O*NET)-Standard Occupational Classification System (SOC) index. The DOT, GOE, and O*NET-SOC indexes have been created by the U.S. government; the NOC index is Canada's career classification system. Readers can use the identification numbers listed in the Quick Facts section to access further information on a career. Print editions of the DOT (*Dictionary of Occupational Titles.* Indianapolis, Ind.: JIST Works, 1991) and GOE (*The Complete Guide for Occupational Exploration.* Indianapolis, Ind.: JIST Works, 1993) are available at libraries, and electronic versions of the NOC (http://www23.hrdc-drhc.gc.ca/2001/e/generic/welcome.shtml) and O*NET-SOC (http://online.onetcenter.org) are available on the World Wide Web. When no DOT, GOE, NOC, or O*NET-SOC numbers are present, this means that the U.S. Department of Labor or the Human Resources Development Canada have not created a numerical designation for this career. In this instance, you will see the acronym "N/A," or not available.

The **Overview** section is a brief introductory description of the duties and responsibilities of someone in the career. Oftentimes, a career may have a variety of job titles. When this is the case, alternative career titles are presented in this section.

The **History** section describes the history of the particular job as it relates to the overall development of its industry or field.

The Job describes the primary and secondary duties of the job.

Requirements discusses high school and postsecondary education and training requirements, any certification or licensing necessary, and any other personal requirements for success in the job.

Exploring offers suggestions on how to gain some experience in or knowledge of the particular job before making a firm educational and financial commitment. The focus is on what can be done while still in high school (or in the early years of college) to gain a better understanding of the job.

The **Employers** section gives an overview of typical places of employment for the job.

Starting Out discusses the best ways to land that first job, be it through the college placement office, newspaper ads, or personal contact.

The **Advancement** section describes what kind of career path to expect from the job and how to get there.

Earnings lists salary ranges and describes the typical fringe benefits.

The **Work Environment** section describes the typical surroundings and conditions of employment, whether indoors or outdoors, noisy or quiet, social or independent, and so on. Also discussed are typical hours worked, any seasonal fluctuations, and the stresses and strains of the job.

The **Outlook** section summarizes the job in terms of the general economy and industry projections. For the most part, Outlook information is obtained from the Bureau of Labor Statistics and is supplemented by information taken from professional associations. Job growth terms follow those used in the Occupational Outlook Handbook: Growth described as "much faster than the average" means an increase of 36 percent or more. Growth described as "faster than the average" means an increase of 21–35 percent. Growth described as "about as fast as the average" means an increase of 10–20 percent. Growth described as "little change or more slowly than the average" means an increase of 0–9 percent. "Decline" means a decrease of 1 percent or more.

Each article ends with **For More Information**, which lists organizations that can provide career information on training, education, internships, scholarships, and job placement. Throughout the book you will also find helpful sidebars, interviews with professionals working in the field, and illustrative photos of several careers.

The field of clerical and administrative work offers a wide variety of opportunities to suit many different interests. This book provides a comprehensive overview of these careers and abundant information to help you prepare for work of this nature.

Billing Clerks

QUICK FACTS

School Subjects
Business
English
Mathematics

Personal Skills
Following instructions
Technical/scientific

Work Environment
Primarily indoors
Primarily one location

Minimum Education Level
High school diploma

Salary Range
$17,780 to $25,350 to
$36,490+

Certification or Licensing
None available

Outlook
Little change or more slowly
than the average

DOT
214

GOE
07.02.04

NOC
1431

O*NET-SOC
43-3021.00, 43-3021.02,
43-3021.03

OVERVIEW

Billing clerks produce and process bills and collect payments from customers. They enter transactions in business ledgers or spreadsheets, write and send invoices, and verify purchase orders. They are responsible for posting items in accounts payable or receivable, calculating customer charges, and verifying the company's rates for certain products and services. Billing clerks must make sure that all entries are accurate and up-to-date. At the end of the fiscal year, they may work with auditors to clarify billing procedures and answer questions about specific accounts. There are approximately 506,000 billing clerks employed in the United States.

HISTORY

The need to record business transactions has existed ever since people began to engage in business and commerce. As far back as 3000 B.C., Sumerians in Mesopotamia recorded sales and bills for customers on clay tablets. Wealthy traders of early Egyptian and Babylonian civilizations often used slaves to make markings on clay tablets to keep track of purchases and sales.

With the rise of monarchies in Europe, billing clerks were needed to record the business transactions of kings, queens, and rich merchants and to monitor the status of the royal treasury. During the Middle Ages, monks carried out the tasks of billing clerks. As the Industrial Revolution spread across Europe, increasing commercial transactions, billing clerks became a necessary part of the workforce.

Computer technology has changed the way clerks record transactions today, enabling billing information and financial transactions to be recorded electronically, eliminating the need for paperwork. But billing clerks continue to occupy a central role in the business world, managing the day-to-day inner workings of company finance.

THE JOB

Billing clerks are responsible for keeping records and up-to-date accounts of all business transactions. They type and send bills for services or products and update files to reflect payments. They also review incoming invoices to ensure that the requested products have been delivered and that the billing statements are accurate and paid on time.

Billing clerks set up shipping and receiving dates. They check customer orders before shipping to make sure they are complete and that all costs, shipping charges, taxes, and credits are included. Billing clerks are also troubleshooters. They contact suppliers or customers when payments are past due or incorrect and help solve the minor problems that invariably occur in the course of business transactions.

Billing clerks enter all transaction information onto the firm's account ledger. This ledger lists all the company's transactions such as items bought or sold as well as the credit terms and payment and receiving dates. As payments come in, the billing clerk applies credit and any applicable discounts to customer accounts. All correspondence is carefully filed for future reference. Nearly all of this work is currently done using spreadsheets and computer databases.

The specific duties of billing clerks vary according to the nature of the business in which they work. In an insurance company, the transaction sheet will reflect when and how much customers must pay on their insurance bills. Billing clerks in hospitals compile itemized charges, calculate insurance benefits, and process insurance claims. In accounting, law, and consulting firms, they calculate billable hours and work completed.

Billing clerks are also often responsible for preparing summary statements of financial status, profit-and-loss statements, and payroll lists and deductions. These reports are submitted periodically to company management, who can then gauge the company's financial performance. Clerks may also write company checks, compute federal tax reports, and tabulate personnel profit shares.

Billing clerks may work with several departments in an organization or they can have a specific role. These areas of specialization include the following:

- *Invoice-control clerks* post items in accounts payable or receivable ledgers and verify the accuracy of billing data.

- *Passenger rate clerks* compute fare information for business trips and then provide this information to business personnel.

- COD *(cash-on-delivery) clerks* calculate and record the amount of money collected on COD delivery routes.

- *Interline clerks* compute and pay freight charges for airlines or other transportation agencies that carry freight or passengers as part of a business transaction.

- *Settlement clerks* compute and pay shippers for materials forwarded to a company.

- *Billing-control clerks* compute and pay utility companies for services provided.

- *Rate reviewers* compile data relating to utility costs for management officials.

- *Services clerks* compute and pay tariff charges for boats or ships used to transport materials.

- *Foreign clerks* compute duties, tariffs, and price conversions of exported and imported products.

- *Billing-machine operators* mechanically prepare bills and statements.

- *Deposit-refund clerks* prepare bills for utility customers.

- *Raters* calculate premiums to be paid by customers of insurance companies.

- *Telegraph-service raters* compute costs for sending telegrams.

Billing clerks may work in one specific area or they may be responsible for several areas.

REQUIREMENTS

High School

A high school diploma is usually sufficient for a beginning billing clerk, although business courses in computer operations and bookkeeping are also helpful. In high school, take English, communications, and business-writing courses. Computer science and mathematics courses will

Did You Know?

According to a recent study of businesses with less than $5 million in sales, 53 percent said their companies currently outsource one or more traditional office procedures. The study also found that the most common areas for outsourcing are payroll, patient billing, administration of employee benefits, and maintenance services.

Source: Claim Kare Solutions (http://www.claimkaresolutions.com)

also be helpful. Some companies test their applicants on math, typing, and computer skills, and others offer on-the-job training.

Postsecondary Training
Community colleges, junior colleges, and vocational schools often offer business education courses that can provide you with additional training.

Other Requirements
If you hope to be a billing clerk, you should have excellent mathematical and organizational skills, be detail-oriented, and be able to concentrate on repetitive tasks for long periods of time. In addition, you should be dependable, honest, and trustworthy in dealing with confidential financial matters.

EXPLORING
You can gain experience in this field by taking on clerical or bookkeeping responsibilities with a school club, student government, or other extracurricular activities. If you are interested in the field, you can work in retail operations, either part time or during the summer. Working at the cash register or even pricing products as a stockperson is a good introductory experience. It also may be possible to gain some experience by volunteering to help maintain the bookkeeping records for local groups, such as churches and small businesses.

EMPLOYERS
Employers of billing clerks include hospitals, insurance companies, banks, manufacturers, and utility companies. Of the approximately

506,000 billing clerks employed in the United States, roughly one-third work in the health care field.

STARTING OUT

Your high school job placement or guidance office can help you find employment opportunities or establish job contacts after you graduate. You may also find specific jobs through classified newspaper advertisements. Most companies provide on-the-job training for entry-level billing clerks in order to explain to them company procedures and policies and to teach them the basic tasks of the job. During the first month, billing clerks work with experienced personnel.

ADVANCEMENT

Billing clerks usually begin by handling routine tasks such as recording transactions. With experience, they may advance to more complex assignments—which entail computer training in databases and spreadsheets—and assume a greater responsibility for the work as a whole. With additional training and education, billing clerks can be promoted to positions as bookkeepers, accountants, or auditors. Billing clerks with strong leadership and management skills can advance to group manager or supervisor.

There is a high turnover rate in this field, which increases the chance of promotion for employees with ability and initiative.

EARNINGS

Salaries for billing clerks depend on the size and geographic location of the company and the employee's skills. Record clerks (which include the position of billing clerks) who work for the federal government earn starting salaries of about $18,000. Full-time billing and posting clerks earned a median hourly wage of $12.19 in 2001, according to the U.S. Department of Labor (DOL). For full-time work at 40 hours per week, this hourly wage translates into an annual income of approximately $25,350. The DOL also reported that salaries for these workers ranged from less than $17,780 to more than $36,490. Earnings also vary by responsibilities; for example, the DOL reports that billing clerks responsible for doing purchase orders and keeping track of purchase requests earned a median of $13.33 per hour in 2000. This hourly amount translates into a yearly salary of approximately $27,725 for full-time work. Billing clerks with high levels of expertise and management responsibilities may make more than this amount. Full-time workers also receive paid vacation, health insurance, and other benefits.

WORK ENVIRONMENT

Like most office workers, billing clerks usually work in modern office environments and average 37–40 hours of work per week. Billing clerks spend most of their time behind a desk, and their work can be routine and repetitive. Working long hours in front of a computer can often cause eyestrain, backaches, and headaches, although efforts are being made to reduce physical problems with ergonomically correct equipment. Billing clerks should enjoy systematic and orderly work and have a keen eye for numerical detail. While much of the work is solitary, billing clerks often interact with accountants and management and may work under close supervision.

OUTLOOK

The U.S. Department of Labor predicts that opportunities for billing clerks will grow more slowly than the average over the next several years. A number of factors contribute to this slow growth rate. For example, technological advancements—computers, electronic billing, and automated payment methods—will streamline operations and result in the need for fewer workers. Additionally, the responsibilities of billing clerks may be combined with those of other positions. In smaller companies, for example, accounting clerks will make use of billing software, making billing clerks obsolete. Many job openings will result from the need to replace workers who have left for different jobs or other reasons. The health care sector should remain a large employer in this field.

FOR MORE INFORMATION

For additional career information, contact:
Office and Professional Employees International Union
265 West 14th Street, 6th Floor
New York, NY 10011
Tel: 800-346-7348
Email: opeiu@opeiu.org
http://www.opeiu.org

Bookkeeping and Accounting Clerks

QUICK FACTS

School Subjects
Business
Computer science
Mathematics

Personal Skills
Following instructions
Technical/scientific

Work Environment
Primarily indoors
Primarily one location

Minimum Education Level
High school diploma

Salary Range
$17,120 to $26,540 to
$40,790+

Certification or Licensing
None available

Outlook
Little change or more slowly
than the average

DOT
216

GOE
07.02.02

NOC
1431

O*NET-SOC
43-3031.00

OVERVIEW

Bookkeeping and accounting clerks record financial transactions for government, business, and other organizations. They compute, classify, record, and verify numerical data in order to develop and maintain accurate financial records. There are approximately 2 million bookkeeping, accounting, and auditing clerks employed in the United States.

HISTORY

The history of bookkeeping developed along with the growth of business and industrial enterprise. The first known records of bookkeeping date back to 2600 B.C., when the Babylonians used pointed sticks to mark accounts on clay slabs. By 3000 B.C., Middle Eastern and Egyptian cultures employed a system of numbers to record merchants' transactions of the grain and farm products that were distributed from storage warehouses. The growth of intricate trade systems brought about the necessity for bookkeeping systems.

Sometime after the start of the 13th century, the decimal numeration system was introduced in Europe, simplifying bookkeeping record systems. The merchants of Venice—one of the busiest trading centers in the world at that time—are credited with the invention of the double-entry bookkeeping method that is widely used today.

As industry in the United States expands and grows more complex, simpler and quicker bookkeeping methods and procedures have evolved. Technological developments include bookkeeping machines, computer hardware and software, and electronic data processing.

THE JOB

Bookkeeping workers keep systematic records and current accounts of financial transactions for businesses, institutions, industries, charities, and other organizations. The bookkeeping records of a firm or business are a vital part of its operational procedures because these records reflect the assets and the liabilities, as well as the profits and losses, of the operation.

Bookkeepers record these business transactions daily in spreadsheets on computer databases, and accounting clerks often input the information. The practice of posting accounting records directly onto ledger sheets, in journals, or on other types of written accounting forms is decreasing as computerized record-keeping becomes more widespread. In small businesses, bookkeepers sort and record all the sales slips, bills, check stubs, inventory lists, and requisition lists. They compile figures for cash receipts, accounts payable and receivable, and profits and losses.

Accountants set up bookkeeping systems and use bookkeepers' balance sheets to prepare periodic summary statements of financial transactions. Management relies heavily on these bookkeeping records to interpret the organization's overall performance and uses them to make important business decisions. The records are also necessary to file income tax reports and prepare quarterly reports for stockholders.

Accounting clerks handle the clerical accounting work; they enter and verify transaction data and compute and record various charges. They may also monitor loans and accounts payable and receivable. More advanced clerks may reconcile billing vouchers, while senior workers review invoices and statements.

Bookkeeping and accounting clerks work in retail and wholesale businesses, manufacturing firms, hospitals, schools, charities, and other types of institutional agencies. Many clerks are classified as financial institution bookkeeping and accounting clerks, insurance firm bookkeeping and accounting clerks, hotel bookkeeping and accounting clerks, and railroad bookkeeping and accounting clerks.

General bookkeepers and *general-ledger bookkeepers* are usually employed in smaller business operations. They may perform all the analysis, maintain the financial records, and complete any other tasks that are involved in keeping a full set of bookkeeping records. These employees may have other general office duties, such as mailing state-

A bookkeeping clerk sorts through the records of one her company's clients. *(Tomas del Amo/FlashFocus)*

ments, answering telephone calls, and filing materials. *Audit clerks* verify figures and may be responsible for sending them on to an audit clerk supervisor.

In large companies, an accountant may supervise a department of bookkeepers who perform more specialized work. *Billing and rate clerks* and *fixed capital clerks* may post items in accounts payable or receivable ledgers, make out bills and invoices, or verify the company's rates for certain products and services. *Account information clerks* prepare reports, compile payroll lists and deductions, write company checks, and compute federal tax reports or personnel profit shares. Large companies may employ workers to organize, record, and compute many other types of financial information.

In large business organizations, bookkeepers and accountants may be classified by grades, such as Bookkeeper I or II. The job classification determines their responsibilities.

REQUIREMENTS

High School

Bookkeepers need to have at least a high school diploma. A background in business mathematics, business writing, typing, and computer training is particularly helpful in this career. Developing sound English, communication, and mathematical skills is also very important.

Postsecondary Training

Some employers prefer people who have completed a junior college curriculum or those who have attended a post-high-school business training program. In many instances, employers offer on-the-job training for various types of entry-level positions. In some areas, work-study programs are available in which schools, in cooperation with businesses, offer part-time, practical on-the-job training combined with academic study. These programs often help students find immediate employment in similar work after graduation. Local business schools may also offer evening courses.

Other Requirements

Bookkeepers need strong mathematical skills and organizational abilities, and they have to be able to concentrate on detailed work. The work is quite sedentary and often tedious, and you should not mind long hours behind a desk. You should be methodical, accurate, and orderly and enjoy working on detailed tasks. Employers look for honest, discreet, and trustworthy individuals when placing their business in someone else's hands.

Once you are employed as a bookkeeping and accounting clerk, some places of business may require you to have union membership. Larger unions include the Office and Professional Employees International Union; the International Union of Electronics, Electrical, Salaried, Machine, and Furniture Workers; and the American Federation of State, County, and Municipal Employees. Also, depending on the business, clerks may be represented by the same union as other manufacturing employees.

EXPLORING

You can gain experience in bookkeeping by participating in work-study programs or by obtaining part-time or summer work in beginning bookkeeping jobs or related office work. Any retail experience dealing with cash management, pricing, or customer service is also valuable.

You can also volunteer to manage the books for extracurricular student groups. Managing income or cash flow for a club or acting as treasurer for student government are excellent ways to gain experience in maintaining financial records.

Other options are visiting local small businesses to observe their work and talking to representatives of schools that offer business training courses.

EMPLOYERS

Of the approximately 2 million bookkeeping, auditing, and accounting clerks, many work for personnel supplying companies; that is, those companies that provide part-time or temporary office workers. Approximately 25 percent of bookkeeping and accounting clerks work part time, according to the U.S. Department of Labor. Many others are employed by government agencies and organizations that provide educational, health, business, and social services.

STARTING OUT

You may find jobs or establish contacts with businesses that are interested in interviewing graduates through your guidance or placement offices. A work-study program or internship may result in a full-time job offer. Business schools and junior colleges generally provide assistance to their graduates in locating employment.

You may locate job opportunities by applying directly to firms or responding to ads in newspaper classified sections. State employment agencies and private employment bureaus can also assist in the job-search process.

ADVANCEMENT

Bookkeeping workers generally begin their employment by performing routine tasks, such as the simple recording of transactions. Beginners may start as entry-level clerks, cashiers, bookkeeping machine operators, office assistants, or typists. With experience, they may advance to more complex assignments that include computer training in databases and spreadsheets and assume a greater responsibility for the work as a whole.

With experience and education, clerks become department heads or office managers. Further advancement to positions such as office or division manager, department head, accountant, or auditor is possible with a college degree and years of experience. There is a high turnover rate in this field, which increases the promotion opportunities for employees with ability and initiative.

EARNINGS

According to the U.S. Department of Labor, bookkeepers and accounting clerks earned a median income of $26,540 a year in 2001. Earnings are also influenced by such factors as the size of the city where they work and the size and type of business for which they are employed. Clerks just starting out earn approximately $17,120. Those with one or two years of college generally earn higher starting wages. Top-paying jobs average about $40,790 a year.

Employees usually receive six to eight paid holidays yearly and one week of paid vacation after six to 12 months of service. Paid vacations may increase to four weeks or more, depending on length of service and place of employment. Fringe benefits may include health and life insurance, sick leave, and retirement plans.

WORK ENVIRONMENT

The majority of office workers, including bookkeeping workers, usually work a 40-hour week, although some employees may work a 35–37-hour week. Bookkeeping and accounting clerks usually work in typical office settings. They are more likely to have a cubicle than an office. While the work pace is steady, it can also be routine and repetitive, especially in large companies where the employee is often assigned only one or two specialized job duties.

Attention to numerical details can be physically demanding, and the work can produce eyestrain and nervousness. While bookkeepers usually work with other people and sometimes under close supervision, they can expect to spend most of their day behind a desk; this may seem confining to people who need more variety and stimulation in their work. In addition, the constant attention to detail and the need for accuracy can place considerable responsibility on the worker and cause much stress.

OUTLOOK

Even though the demands placed on accountants and clerks have increased over the past several years, the automation of office functions will continue to improve overall worker productivity. Fewer people will be needed to do the work, and employment of bookkeeping and accounting clerks is expected to show little change over the next several years, according to the U.S. Department of Labor. Excellent computer skills will be vital to securing a job.

Despite lack of growth, there will be numerous replacement job openings, since the turnover rate in this occupation is high. Offices are centralizing their operations, often setting up one center to manage all accounting needs in a single location. As more companies trim back their workforces, opportunities for temporary work should continue to grow.

FOR MORE INFORMATION

For information on accredited educational programs, contact:
Association to Advance Collegiate Schools of Business
600 Emerson Road, Suite 300
St. Louis, MO 63141-6762
Tel: 314-872-8481
http://www.aacsb.edu

For more information on women in accounting, contact:
Educational Foundation for Women in Accounting
PO Box 1925
Southeastern, PA 19399-1925
Tel: 610-407-9229
Email: info@efwa.org
http://www.efwa.org

Collection Workers

OVERVIEW

Collection workers—sometimes known as *bill collectors, collection correspondents,* or *collection agents*—are employed to persuade people to pay their overdue bills. Some work for collection agencies (which are hired by the business to which the money is owed), while others work for department stores, hospitals, banks, public utilities, and other businesses. Collection workers contact delinquent debtors, inform them of the delinquency, and either secure payment or arrange a new payment schedule. If all else fails, they might be forced to repossess property or turn the account over to an attorney for legal proceedings. There are approximately 400,000 collection workers employed in the United States.

HISTORY

Debt collection is one of the world's oldest vocations. In literature, the most famous—and unsuccessful—attempt to retrieve an overdue debt occurred in Shakespeare's (1564–1616) *Merchant of Venice,* featuring the character Shylock as the collector. Debt collection also figures prominently in the works of Charles Dickens (1812–70).

In the past, people who were unable to pay their debts suffered great punishments. Some were sent to prison, indentured as servants or slaves until the amount owed was paid off, or recruited by force to colonize new territories. Today's debtors face less harsh consequences, but the proliferation of credit opportunities has expanded the field of debt collection. Charge accounts are now offered by department stores, banks, credit unions, gasoline stations, and other businesses. Many people buy furniture or other expensive

QUICK FACTS

School Subjects
Computer science
Psychology
Speech

Personal Skills
Communication/ideas
Following instructions

Work Environment
Primarily indoors
Primarily one location

Minimum Education Level
High school diploma

Salary Range
$17,960 to $25,960 to $39,030+

Certification or Licensing
Voluntary

Outlook
Faster than the average

DOT
241

GOE
07.04.02

NOC
1435

O*NET-SOC
43-3011.00, 43-4041.00, 43-4041.01, 43-4041.02

items "on time," meaning they place a small sum down and pay off the balance, plus interest, over a certain period of time. People take out mortgages to finance home purchases and auto loans to finance vehicles. The result of all these credit opportunities is that some people take on too much debt and either fail to meet these obligations or refuse to pay them. When creditors do not receive their payments on time, they employ a collection worker to try and recover the money for them.

THE JOB

A collection worker's main job is to persuade people to pay bills that are past due. The procedure is generally the same in both collection firms and businesses that employ collection workers. The duties of the various workers may overlap, depending on the size and nature of the company.

When routine billing methods—monthly statements and notice letters—fail to secure payment, the collection worker receives a bad-debt file (usually on a computer tape downloaded to the agency's computer system). This file contains information about the debtor, the nature and amount of the unpaid bill, the last charge incurred, and the date of the last payment. The collection worker then contacts the debtor by phone or mail to request full or partial payment or, if necessary, to arrange a new payment schedule.

Terrence Sheffert is a collection worker for a collection agency based in Chicago. He describes his typical duties as making phone calls and writing letters. "I am usually in the office, on the phone with clients or the people who owe them," he says. "I never actually go out to make collections, but there are some agents who do."

If the bill has not been paid because the customer believes it is incorrect, the merchandise purchased was faulty, or the service billed for was not performed, the collector takes appropriate steps to settle the matter. If, after investigation, the debt collector finds that the debt is still valid, he or she again tries to secure payment.

In cases where the customer has not paid because of a financial emergency or poor money management, the debt collector may arrange a new payment schedule. In instances where the customer goes to great or fraudulent lengths to avoid payment, the collector may recommend that the file be turned over to an attorney. "Every day, we are protecting the clients' interests and getting the money," Sheffert says. "If we can't get it, then we'll call in legal representation to handle it."

When all efforts to obtain payment fail, a collection worker known as a *repossessor* may be assigned to find the merchandise on which the debtor still owes money and return it to the seller. Such goods as

Collection Facts

- Collection workers must comply with the Fair Debt Collection Practices Act and the Fair Credit Reporting Act.

- There is a Fair Debt Forum at http://www.fairdebtcollection.com.

- You can purchase a Community Education Kit from the Association of Credit and Collection Professionals. The kit is aimed at educational young adults on financial issues, and can be found at http://wwww.acainternational.com.

furniture or appliances can be picked up in a truck. To reclaim automobiles and other motor vehicles, the repossessor might be forced to enter and start the vehicle with special tools if the buyer does not surrender the key.

In large agencies, some collection workers specialize as *skip tracers*. Skip tracers are assigned to find debtors who "skip" out on their debts—that is, who move without notifying their creditors so that they don't have to pay their bills. Skip tracers act like detectives, searching telephone directories and street listings and making inquiries at post offices in an effort to locate missing debtors. Increasingly such information can be found through online computer databases (some agencies subscribe to a service to collect this information). Skip tracers also try to find out information about a person's whereabouts by contacting former neighbors and employers, local merchants, friends, relatives, and references listed on the original credit application. They follow every lead and prepare a report of the entire investigation.

In some small offices, collection workers perform clerical duties, such as reading and answering correspondence, filing, or posting amounts paid to people's accounts. They might offer financial advice to customers or contact them to inquire about their satisfaction with the handling of the account. In larger companies, *credit and loan collection supervisors* might oversee the activities of several other collection workers.

REQUIREMENTS

High School

Most employers prefer to hire high school graduates for collection jobs, but formal education beyond high school is typically not required. High school courses that might prove helpful in this career include those that will help you communicate clearly and properly, such as English and speech. Because collection workers have to talk with people about a very delicate subject, psychology classes might also be beneficial. Finally, computer classes are good choices, since this career, like most others, often requires at least some familiarity with keyboarding and basic computer operation.

Postsecondary Training
Most collection workers learn collection procedures and telephone techniques on the job in a training period spent under the guidance of a supervisor or an experienced collector. The legal restrictions on collection activities, such as when and how calls can be made, are also covered.

Certification or Licensing
Although it is not required by law, some employers require their employees to become certified by the American Collectors Association (ACA). The ACA conducts seminars on state and federal compliance laws that pertain to collection workers. A basic knowledge of legal proceedings is helpful for supervisors. To learn more, visit http://www.collector.com.

Other Requirements
Because this is a people-oriented job, you must have a pleasant manner and voice. You may spend much of your time on the telephone speaking with people about overdue payments, which can be a delicate subject. To succeed as a collector, you must be sympathetic and tactful, yet assertive and persuasive enough to convince debtors to pay their overdue bills. In addition, collectors must be alert, quick-witted, and imaginative to handle the unpredictable and potentially awkward situations that are encountered in this type of work.

Collection work can be emotionally taxing. It involves listening to a bill payer's problems and occasional verbal attacks directed at both the collector and the company. Some people physically threaten repossessors and other collection workers. "The best description of this job would be stressful," Terrence Sheffert says. "Everything about collecting is very stressful." In the face of these stresses, you must be able to avoid becoming upset, personally involved with, or alarmed by angry or threatening debtors. This requires a cool head and an even temperament.

EXPLORING
The best way to explore collection work is to secure part-time or summer employment in a collection agency or credit office. You might

also find it helpful to interview a collection worker to obtain firsthand information about the practical aspects of this occupation. Finally, the associations listed at the end of this article may be able to provide further information about the career.

EMPLOYERS

Of the approximately 400,000 collection workers in the United States, approximately 17 percent work for collection agencies. Collection agencies are usually independent companies that are hired by various businesses to collect debt that is owed them. Other bill collectors work for a wide range of organizations and businesses that extend credit to customers. Department stores, hospitals, banks, public utilities, and auto financing companies are examples of businesses that frequently hire bill collectors.

The companies that hire collection workers are located throughout the United States, especially in heavily populated urban areas. Companies that have branch offices in rural communities often locate their collection departments in nearby cities.

STARTING OUT

Terrence Sheffert got started in collection work because it was a family profession. "My whole family is in collecting, so I thought, 'Hey, I'll go for it,'" he says. If you are interested in becoming a collection worker, one easy way to start a job search is to apply directly to collection agencies, credit reporting companies, banks, and major retailers that sell large items. To find collection agencies and credit reporting companies, try doing a simple keyword search on one of the Internet's search engines. Another easy way is to look in your local Yellow Pages—or expand your search by going to the library and looking through yellow pages of other cities. Remember that these sorts of jobs are often more plentiful in more urban areas.

You should also check the classified ads of area newspapers for headings such as "Billing" or "Collection." Finally, job openings may be listed at your local employment office.

ADVANCEMENT

Experienced collection workers who have displayed above-average ability can advance to management positions, such as supervisors or *collection managers*. These workers generally have responsibility for the operations of a specific shift, location, or department of a collection company. They oversee other collection workers. Other avenues of advancement might include becoming a *credit authorizer, credit checker,* or *bank loan officer.* Credit authorizers approve questionable charges against customers' existing accounts by evaluating the customers' computerized credit records and payment histories. Credit checkers in credit bureaus—sometimes also called *credit investigators* or *credit reporters*—search for, update, and verify information for credit reports. Loan officers help borrowers fill out loan applications, verify and analyze applications, and decide whether and how much to loan applicants. Some experienced and successful collection workers might open their own agencies. This is Terrence Sheffert's goal. "I hope to advance from collection to management, and then open up my own business," he says.

EARNINGS

Collection workers might receive a salary plus a bonus or commission on the debt amounts they collect. Others work for a flat salary with no commissions. Since the pay system varies among different companies, incomes vary substantially. In 2001, the median hourly wage for bill collectors working full time was $12.48, according to the U.S. Department of Labor. This hourly wage translates into a yearly income of approximately $25,960. Earnings for collection workers range from less than $17,960 to a high of more than $39,030 annually.

Depending on their employer, some full-time bill collectors receive a benefits package that may include paid holidays and vacations, sick leave, and health and dental insurance.

WORK ENVIRONMENT

Most collectors work in pleasant offices, sit at a desk, and spend a great deal of time on the telephone. Because they spend so much time on the phone, many collectors use phone headsets and program-operated dialing systems. Because most companies use computers to store information about their accounts, the collection worker frequently works on a computer. He or she may sit in front of a computer terminal, reviewing and entering information about the account while talking to the debtor on the phone.

Rarely does a collector have to make a personal visit to a customer. Repossession proceedings are undertaken only in extreme cases.

Terrence Sheffert works a 40-hour week, from 9:00 A.M. to 5:00 P.M., Monday through Friday. Some collection workers stagger their schedules, however. They might start late in the morning and work into the evening, or they might take a weekday off and work on Saturday. Evening and weekend work is common, because debtors are often home during these times.

OUTLOOK

The U.S. Department of Labor Employment predicts faster than the average over the next several years for bill collectors. This demand is due in part to the relaxed standards for credit cards, which means more people, regardless of their financial circumstances, are able to get credit cards, make purchases on credit, and build up large debts they have difficulty repaying. The Department of Labor also notes that hospitals and physicians' offices are two of the fastest growing employers of bill collectors and collection agencies. This is largely because health insurance plans frequently do not adequately cover payment for medical procedures, and patients are often left with large bills that they have difficulty repaying. Economic recessions also increase the amount of personal debt that goes unpaid. Therefore, unlike many occupations, collection workers usually find that their employment and workloads increase during economic slumps.

FOR MORE INFORMATION

For a brochure on careers in collection work, contact:
Association of Credit and Collection Professionals
PO Box 390106
Minneapolis, MN 55439
Tel: 952-926-6547
http://www.acainternational.org

For information on careers and certification, contact the NACM:
National Association of Credit Management (NACM)
8840 Columbia 100 Parkway
Columbia, MD 21045
Tel: 410-740-5560
Email: nacm_info@nacm.org
http://www.nacm.org

Counter and Retail Clerks

QUICK FACTS

School Subjects
English
Mathematics
Speech

Personal Skills
Following instructions
Helping/teaching

Work Environment
Primarily indoors
Primarily one location

Minimum Education Level
High school diploma

Salary Range
$12,240 to $16,750 to
$29,720+

Certification or Licensing
None available

Outlook
About as fast as the average

DOT
279

GOE
08.02.03

NOC
1453

O*NET-SOC
41-2021.00

OVERVIEW

Counter and retail clerks work as intermediaries between the general public and businesses that provide goods and services. They take orders and receive payments for such services as videotape rentals, automobile rentals, and laundry and dry cleaning. They often assist customers with their purchasing or rental decisions, especially when sales personnel are not available. These workers might also prepare billing statements, keep records of receipts and sales, and balance money in their cash registers.

HISTORY

The first retail outlets in the United States sold food staples, farm necessities, and clothing, and many also served as the post office and became the social and economic centers of their communities. Owners of these general stores often performed all the jobs in the business.

Over the years retailing has undergone numerous changes. Large retail stores, requiring many workers, including counter and retail clerks, became more common. Also emerging were specialized retail or chain outlets—clothing stores, bicycle shops, computer shops, video stores, and athletic footwear boutiques—that also needed counter and retail clerks to assist customers and to receive payment for services or products.

THE JOB

Job duties vary depending on the type of business. In a shoe repair shop, for example, the clerk receives the shoes to be repaired or

24

cleaned from the customer, examines the shoes, gives a price quote and a receipt to the customer, and then sends the shoes to the work department for the necessary repairs or cleaning. The shoes are marked with a tag specifying what work needs to be done and to whom the shoes belong. After the work is completed, the clerk returns the shoes to the customer and collects payment.

In stores where customers rent equipment or merchandise, clerks prepare rental forms and quote rates to customers. The clerks answer customer questions about the operation of the equipment. They often take a deposit to cover any accidents or possible damage. Clerks also check the equipment to be certain it is in good working order and make minor adjustments, if necessary. With long-term rentals, such as storage-facility rentals, clerks notify the customers when the rental period is about to expire and when the rent is overdue. *Video-rental clerks* greet customers, check out tapes, and accept payment. Upon return of the tapes, the clerks check the condition of the tapes and then put them back on the shelves.

In smaller shops with no sales personnel or in situations when the sales personnel are unavailable, counter and retail clerks assist customers with purchases or rentals by demonstrating the merchandise, answering customers' questions, accepting payment, recording sales, and wrapping the purchases or arranging for their delivery.

In addition to these duties, clerks sometimes prepare billing statements to be sent to customers. They might keep records of receipts and sales throughout the day and balance the money in their registers when their work shift ends. They sometimes are responsible for the display and presentation of products in their store. In supermarkets and grocery stores, clerks stock shelves and bag food purchases for the customers.

Service-establishment attendants work in various types of businesses, such as a laundry, where attendants take clothes to be cleaned or repaired and write down the customer's name and address. *Watch-and-clock-repair clerks* receive clocks and watches for repair and examine the timepieces to estimate repair costs. They might make minor repairs, such as replacing a watchband; otherwise, the timepiece is forwarded to the repair shop with a description of needed repairs.

Many clerks have job titles that describe what they do and where they work. These include laundry-pricing clerks, photo-finishing-counter clerks, tool-and-equipment-rental clerks, airplane-charter clerks, baby-stroller and wheelchair-rental clerks, storage-facility-rental clerks, boat-rental clerks, hospital-television-rental clerks, trailer-rental clerks, automobile-rental clerks, fur-storage clerks, and self-service-laundry and dry-cleaning attendants.

A counter clerk describes the cars available for rent. *(Corbis)*

REQUIREMENTS

High School

High school courses useful for the job include English, speech, and mathematics, as well as any business-related classes, such as typing, computer science, and those covering principles in retailing. Although there are no specific educational requirements for clerk positions, most employers prefer to hire high school graduates. Legible handwriting and the ability to add and subtract numbers quickly are also necessary.

Other Requirements

To be a counter and retail clerk, you should have a pleasant personality and an ability to interact with a variety of people. You should also be neat and well groomed and have a high degree of personal responsibility. Counter and retail clerks must be able to adjust to alternating periods of heavy and light activity. No two days—or even customers—are alike. Because some customers can be rude or even hostile, you must exercise tact and patience at all times.

EXPLORING

There are numerous opportunities for part-time or temporary work as a clerk, especially during the holiday season. Many high schools have developed work-study programs that combine courses in retailing with part-time work in the field. Store owners cooperating in these programs may hire you as a full-time worker after you complete the course.

EMPLOYERS

Of the numerous types of clerks working in the United States, approximately 423,000 work as counter and rental clerks at video rental stores, dry cleaners, car rental agencies, and other such establishments. Stock clerks employed by supermarkets and grocery stores hold about 500,000 jobs. These are not the only employers of clerks, however; hardware stores, shoe stores, moving businesses, camera stores—in fact, nearly any business that sells goods or provides services to the general public employs clerks. Many work on a part-time basis.

STARTING OUT

If you are interested in securing an entry-level position as a clerk, you should contact stores directly. Workers with some experience, such as those who have completed a work-study program in high school, should have the greatest success, but most entry-level positions do not require any previous experience. Jobs are often listed in help-wanted advertisements.

Most stores provide new workers with on-the-job training in which experienced clerks explain company policies and procedures and teach new employees how to operate the cash register and other necessary equipment. This training usually continues for several weeks until the new employee feels comfortable on the job.

ADVANCEMENT

Counter and retail clerks usually begin their employment doing routine tasks, such as checking stock and operating the cash register. With experience, they might advance to more complicated assignments and assume some sales responsibilities. Those with the skill and aptitude might become salespeople or store managers, although further education is normally required for management positions.

The high turnover rate in the clerk position increases the opportunities for being promoted. The number and kind of opportunities, however, depend on the place of employment and the ability, training, and experience of the employee.

EARNINGS

According to the U.S. Department of Labor, the median hourly wage for counter and rental clerks was $8.05 in 2001. Working year round at 40 hours per week, a clerk earning this wage would make approximately $16,750 annually. Ten percent of counter and rental clerks earned less than $5.89 per hour (approximately $12,240 annually) in 2001, and 10 percent earned more than $14.29 per hour (or $29,720 annually). Wages among clerks vary for a number of reasons including the industry in which they work. The Department of Labor reports, for example, that those working in the automobile rental field had median hourly earnings of $9.16 (approximately $19,050 per year) in 2000, while those in videotape rentals earned a median of $6.60 per hour (approximately $13,730 yearly). Wages also vary among clerks due to factors such as size of the business, location in the country, and experience of the employee.

Those workers who have union affiliation (usually those who work for supermarkets) may earn considerably more than their nonunion counterparts. Full-time workers, especially those who are union members, might also receive benefits such as paid vacation time and health insurance, but this is not the industry norm. Some businesses offer merchandise discounts for their employees. Part-time workers usually receive fewer benefits than those working full time.

WORK ENVIRONMENT

Although a 40-hour workweek is common, many stores operate on a 44- to 48-hour workweek. Most stores are open on Saturday and many on Sunday. Most stores are also open one or more weekday evenings, so a clerk's working hours might vary from week to week and include evening and weekend shifts. Many counter and retail clerks work overtime during Christmas and other rush seasons. Part-time clerks generally work during peak business periods.

Most clerks work indoors in well-ventilated and well-lighted environments. The job can be routine and repetitive, and clerks often spend much of their time on their feet.

OUTLOOK

The U.S. Department of Labor predicts that employment for counter and rental clerks will grow about as fast as the average over the next several years. Businesses that focus on customer service will always want to hire friendly and responsible clerks. Major employers should be those providing rental products and services, such as car rental firms, video rental stores, and other equipment rental businesses. Because of the high turnover in this field, however, many job openings will come from the need to replace workers. Opportunities for temporary or part-time work should be good, especially during busy business periods. Employment opportunities for clerks are plentiful in large metropolitan areas, where their services are in great demand.

FOR MORE INFORMATION

For information about educational programs in the retail industry, contact:

International Mass Retail Association
1700 North Moore Street, Suite 2250
Arlington, VA 22209
Tel: 703-841-2300
http://www.imra.org

National Retail Federation
325 7th Street, NW, Suite 1100
Washington, DC 20004
Tel: 800-673-4692
http://www.nrf.com

Data Entry Clerks

QUICK FACTS

School Subjects
Business
Computer science
English

Personal Skills
Following instructions
Mechanical/manipulative

Work Environment
Primarily indoors
Primarily one location

Minimum Education Level
High school diploma

Salary Range
$15,640 to $21,960 to
$31,270+

Certification or Licensing
None available

Outlook
Decline

DOT
203

GOE
07.06.01

NOC
1422

O*NET-SOC
43-9021.00

OVERVIEW

Data entry clerks transfer information from paper documents to a computer system. They use either a typewriter-like (alphanumeric) keyboard or a 10-key (numerals only) pad to enter data into the system. In this way, the data is converted into a form the computer can easily read and process. There are about 634,000 data entry and information processing workers in the United States.

HISTORY

Following World War II, the electronic technology that had been used during the war was transferred to government and business sectors for use in peacetime operations. This technology included one of the earliest computers. The first all-purpose electronic digital computer was named ENIAC. Developed at the University of Pennsylvania in 1946, it relied on thousands of vacuum tubes like the ones used in the first television sets and radios. In 1951, UNIVAC became the first computer that could handle large amounts of both numeric and alphabetic data easily.

In the 1960s, the invention of the transistor led to smaller, more powerful computers. Personal computers were introduced in the 1970s. As the computer field continued to produce faster, more efficient, and more powerful computers, the capacity of the machines to read, store, process, and organize information increased dramatically. Since the late 1970s computers have become indispensable to private companies, schools, hospitals, and government agencies, all of which rely on vast amounts of information.

The boom in computerized information processing has created the need for qualified data entry clerks.

THE JOB

Data entry clerks are responsible for entering data into computer systems so that the information can be processed to produce important business documents such as sales reports, billing invoices, mailing lists, and many others. Specific job responsibilities vary according to the type of computer system being used and the nature of the employer. For example, a data entry clerk may enter financial information for use at a bank, merchandising information for use at a store, or scientific information for use at a research laboratory.

From a source document such as a financial statement, data entry clerks type in information in alphabetic, numeric, or symbolic code. The information is entered using a keyboard, either the regular typewriter-like computer keyboard or a more customized keypad developed for a certain industry or business. The entry machine converts the coded information into either electronic impulses or a series of holes in a tape that the computer can read and process electronically. Newer, more sophisticated computers have eliminated the need for magnetic tapes, however, and rely exclusively on computer files. Some data entry work does not involve inputting actual information but rather entering special instructions that tell the computer what functions to perform and when to perform them.

In small companies, data entry clerks may combine data entry responsibilities with general office work. Because of staff limitations, clerks may have to know and be able to operate several types of computer systems. Larger companies tend to assign data entry clerks to one type of entry machinery. For example, data entry clerks in a check or credit processing center might be assigned solely to changing client addresses in the company database or entering payment amounts from individual checks.

Some data entry clerks are responsible for setting up their entry machines according to the type of input data. Clerks who handle vast amounts of financial data, for example, set their machines to automatically record a series of numbers as dollar amounts or transaction dates without having to input dollar signs or hyphens. The special setups reduce the number of key strokes necessary to finish one transaction, thereby increasing productivity. Some data entry clerks may be responsible for loading the appropriate tape or other material into their machines and selecting the correct coding system (that is, the alphabetic, numeric, or symbolic representations).

Accuracy is an essential element of all data entry work. If a customer pays $100 toward a credit card bill but the clerk records a payment of only $10, the company will experience problems down the line. Therefore, most companies have an extensive series of accuracy checks and error tests designed to detect as many errors as possible. Some tests are computerized, checking entries against information that is expected for the given type of work or is scanned in directly from source documents. Data entry clerks must always verify their own work as well. They consistently check their computer screens for obvious errors and systematically refer back to the source documents to ensure that they entered the information correctly. Sometimes *verifier operators* are employed specifically to perform accuracy tests of previously processed information. Such tests may be random or complete, depending on the nature and scope of the work. When verifier operators find mistakes, they correct them and later prepare accuracy reports for each data entry clerk.

Data typists and *keypunch operators* formerly prepared data for computer input by punching data into special coding cards or paper tapes. The cards were punched on machines that resembled typewriters. When tapes were used, the work was done on machines such as bookkeeping or adding machines that had special attachments to perforate paper tape. The use of cards and tape is decreasing substantially as electronic databases become more flexible, fast, and efficient. Consequently, most data typists and keypunch operators perform work at terminals similar to those of other data entry clerks.

Data-coder operators examine the information in the source material to determine what codes and symbols should be used to enter it into the computer. They may write the operating instructions for the data entry staff and assist the system programmer in testing and revising computer programs designed to process data entry work. Data-coder operators might also assist programmers in preparing detailed flowcharts of how the information is being stored and used in the computer system and in designing coded computer instructions to fulfill business needs.

Terminal operators also use coding systems to input information from the source document into a series of alphabetic or numeric signals that can be read by the computer. After checking their work for accuracy, they send the data to the computer system via telephone lines or other remote-transmission methods if they do not input directly into the computer network.

How to Get Involved in Data Entry

- Start a student chapter of the Association for Computing Machinery. See http://www.acm.org for details.

- Get a part-time or temporary summer job in an office setting

- Read about the last computing trends in magazines such as Ubiquity (http://www.acm.org/ubiquity).

- Increase your familiarity and comfort level with computers and other office machinery.

REQUIREMENTS

High School

In high school, you should take English, typing, computer science, and other business courses that focus on the operation of office machinery. A high school diploma is usually required for data entry work. In a growing number of cases, some college training is desirable. Most data entry clerks receive on-the-job training pertaining specifically to the computer system and input procedures used by the employer. Before you begin your first job as a data entry clerk, you should be able to quickly scan documents and type the information you read.

Postsecondary Training

Many aspiring data entry clerks now complete data processing courses that instruct students on proper inputting methods and other skills needed for the job. Technical schools, community colleges, business schools, and some adult education programs offer courses related to data processing. These courses are generally between six months and two years in duration. Secretarial or business schools may also offer data entry courses.

Other Requirements

Most companies test prospective employees to evaluate their typing skills in terms of both speed and accuracy. Competency in general mathematics and spelling is frequently reviewed as well. You must be accurate and highly productive, capable of inputting several hundred pieces of information per hour, and you must be comfortable with the high degree of routine and repetition involved in your daily tasks. As computers continue to change, you must always be ready to learn new methods and techniques of input.

EXPLORING

If you are interested in pursuing a career in data entry, you should discuss the field with individuals who are already employed as clerks. A visit to an office that uses data processing systems may provide a good opportunity to learn more about the rewards and drawbacks of this position. Secretarial work or similar office work may also help you understand what data entry work involves. At home or school, you can practice typing by using a computer or typewriter or by entering data for various club or group activities.

EMPLOYERS

Approximately 634,000 data entry clerks are employed in the United States. Of these workers, about 405,000 are data entry keyers and 229,000 are word processors and typists. Major employers of data entry clerks include insurance companies, utilities, banks, credit or check clearinghouses, mail-order catalogs, temporary employment agencies, and manufacturing firms. The federal government operates its own training program for data entry clerks. Applications for such positions may be made through the Office of Personnel Management.

STARTING OUT

Many people entering the field have already completed an educational program at a technical school or other institution that provides data processing training. Job placement counselors at these schools are often very helpful in locating employment opportunities for qualified applicants.

Local and state employment offices as well as classified advertisements list job openings. You may also make direct contact with area employers with data processing departments.

ADVANCEMENT

Data entry positions are considered entry-level jobs, and as such, data entry itself does not offer tremendous potential for growth. Data entry clerks may be promoted to working on more complicated machines or systems, but the work is basically the same. Better opportunities arise when data entry clerks use their computer experience and training to springboard to higher level positions. For example, skilled data entry clerks may be promoted to supervisory positions in which they are responsible for overseeing the data processing department or a team of clerks.

EARNINGS

According to OfficeTeam's *2002 Salary Guide,* salaries for data entry specialists ranged from $19,500 to $23,500. The survey also found that senior data entry specialists earned between $22,000 and $26,000 per year.

The median annual income for data entry clerks in 2001 was $21,960, according to the U.S. Department of Labor. The Department also reported that, at the low end of the scale, 10 percent of data entry workers earned $15,640 or less. The highest paid 10 percent earned $31,270 or more. Salaries for these workers can vary depending on their employer, the complexity of their job duties, and their level of training. In addition, incomes tend to vary by region, with salaries in the western United States being the highest. Salaries for federal and local government employees are comparable to those in the private sector. Full-time and some part-time employees can expect benefits such as medical insurance, sick leave, and paid vacation.

WORK ENVIRONMENT

Most data entry clerks work 37–40 hours per week, with part-time positions becoming increasingly popular. Data entry workstations are usually located in comfortable, well-lighted areas. Data entry clerks must be able to work side by side with other employees and, in most cases, under close supervision. The work is routine, repetitious, and fast-paced and demands the constant, concentrated use of eyes and hands.

The continuous need for accuracy may be stressful to an individual unaccustomed to such working conditions. Duties may require lifting, reaching, and moving boxes of cards, tape, or other materials. Data entry personnel sit for long hours at a time. Long exposure to computer monitors at close range may strain the eyes, and constant use of the hands for typing may lead to nerve or muscle problems, such as carpal tunnel syndrome.

OUTLOOK

Because of improvements in data-processing technology that enable businesses to process greater volumes of information with fewer workers, the U.S. Department of Labor predicts that the employment outlook for data entry clerks is expected to decline over the next several years. Jobs are becoming limited, for example, because many computer systems can now send information directly to another computer system without the need for a data entry clerk to input the information a second time. In addition, the widespread use of personal computers, which permit numerous employees to enter data directly, have also diminished the need for skilled entry personnel. Computer scanners, which read handwritten and typewritten information directly from source documents, and voice recognition technology are making data entry clerks obsolete. More businesses are also contracting temporary and staffing services instead of hiring full-time data entry clerks. Despite these advances in technology, the need for data entry clerks will continue in some businesses.

Even though there will be a slowdown in new job openings for data entry clerks, the high turnover rate due to current employees retiring or receiving job promotions will result in steady job opportunities. Those with the most advanced skills and the ability to adapt to the changing needs of the computer processing field will stand the best chance for continued employment. Job opportunities will be greatest in and around large metropolitan areas, where most banks, insurance and utilities companies, and government agencies are located.

Knowledge of different computer systems and general computer science enhances a data entry clerk's desirability for employers. The ability to work on different systems, particularly specialty systems such as page layout programs and typesetting programs, offers the clerk greater job flexibility.

FOR MORE INFORMATION

For more information on the data entry field, contact:
Association for Computing Machinery
One Astor Plaza
1515 Broadway, 17th Floor
New York, NY 10036-5701
Tel: 212-869-7440
Email: SIGS@acm.org
http://www.acm.org

For a brochure about careers in data processing and information about student chapters, contact:
Association of Information Technology Professionals
401 North Michigan Avenue, Suite 2200
Chicago, IL 60611-4267
Tel: 800-224-9371
Email: aitp_hq@aitp.org
http://www.aitp.org

Financial Institution Tellers, Clerks, and Related Workers

OVERVIEW

Financial institution tellers, clerks, and related workers perform many tasks in banks and other savings institutions. Tellers work at teller windows where they receive and pay out money, record customer transactions, cash checks, sell traveler's checks, and perform other banking duties. The most familiar teller is the *commercial teller,* who works with customers, handling check cashing, deposits, and withdrawals. Specialized tellers are also employed, especially at large financial institutions. Clerks' and related workers' jobs usually vary with the size of the institution. In small banks, a clerk or related worker may perform a combination of tasks, while in larger banks an employee may be assigned to one specialized duty. All banking activities are concerned with the safekeeping, exchange, record-keeping, and credit use of money. There are approximately 499,000 tellers employed in the United States.

HISTORY

The profession of banking is nearly as old as civilization itself. Ancient records show that Babylonian people, for example, had a fairly complex system of lending, borrowing, and depositing money even before 2500 B.C. Other early literature makes reference to "money-lenders" and "money-changers" as ancient writers and travelers described

School Subjects
Business
Computer science
Mathematics

Personal Skills
Following instructions
Mechanical/manipulative

Work Environment
Primarily indoors
Primarily one location

Minimum Education Level
Some postsecondary training

Salary Range
$15,000 to $19,830 to
$26,610+

Certification or Licensing
None available

Outlook
Decline (financial institution tellers)
Little change or more slowly than the average (financial institution clerks and related workers)

DOT
216

GOE
N/A

NOC
1434

O*NET-SOC
43-3021.01, 43-3031.00, 43-3071.00, 43-5021.00

how they bought money in other countries by trading coins from their own homelands.

The term "bank" is derived from the Italian *banco,* meaning bench. Since the time of the Roman Empire, Italy has been an important trading and shipping nation. In medieval times, bankers set up benches on the streets and from these conducted their business of trading currencies and accepting precious metals and jewels for safekeeping. They also lent money at interest to finance the new ventures of shipping merchants and other businesses. Italian cities eventually established permanent banks, and this practice gradually spread north throughout Europe. During the 17th century important banking developments took place in England, which by that time had become a major trading nation. In 1694, the Bank of England was founded in London.

In the United States the Continental Congress chartered the Bank of North America in 1782 in Philadelphia. The first state bank was chartered in Boston in 1784 as the Bank of Massachusetts. Although the development of banking in the United States has experienced periods of slow growth and numerous failures throughout history, Congress and the federal government have done a great deal to make the nation's banking system safer and more effective.

Today, banking, like many other professions, has turned to the use of automation, mechanization, computers, telecommunications, and many modern methods of bookkeeping and record systems. For all the modern banking conveniences that Americans enjoy today, banks and savings institutions employ thousands of workers so that they can offer these services.

THE JOB

Several different types of tellers may work at a financial institution, depending on its size. The teller the average bank customer has the most contact with is the commercial teller, also known as a *paying and receiving teller.* These tellers service the public directly by accepting customers' deposits and providing them with receipts, paying out withdrawals and recording the transactions, cashing checks, exchanging money for customers to provide them with certain kinds of change or currency, and accepting savings account deposits. At the beginning of the workday, each teller is given a cash drawer from the vault containing a certain amount of cash. During the day, this is the money they use for transactions with customers. Their work with the money and their record-keeping must be accurate. At the end of their shifts, the tellers' cash drawers are recounted, and the amount must match up with the transactions done that day. A teller who has problems balancing his or her drawer won't be employed for very long.

Head tellers and *teller supervisors* train tellers, arrange work schedules, and monitor the tellers' records of the day's transactions. If there are any problems in balancing the cash drawers, the head teller or supervisor must try to figure out where the error occurred and reconcile the differences.

At large financial institutions, tellers may perform specialized duties and are identified by the transactions they handle. *Note tellers,* for example, are responsible for receiving and issuing receipts or payments on promissory notes and recording these transactions correctly. *Discount tellers* are responsible for issuing and collecting customers' notes. *Foreign banknote tellers* work in the exchange department, where they buy and sell foreign currency. When customers need to trade their foreign currency for U.S. currency, these tellers determine the current value of the foreign currency in dollars, count out the bills requested by the customer, and make change. These tellers may also sell foreign currency and traveler's checks for people traveling out of the country. *Collection and exchange tellers* accept payments in forms other than cash—contracts, mortgages, and bonds, for example.

While tellers' work involves much interaction with the public, most of the work done by clerks and other related workers is completed behind the scenes. Clerks and related workers are responsible for keeping depositors' money safe, the bank's investments healthy, and government regulations satisfied. All such workers assist in processing the vast amounts of paperwork that a bank generates. This paperwork may consist of deposit slips, checks, financial statements to customers, correspondence, record transactions, and reports for internal and external use. Depending on their job responsibilities, clerks may prepare, collect, send, index, or file these documents. In addition, they may talk with customers and other banks, take telephone calls, and perform other general office duties.

The tasks clerks and related workers perform also depend on the size of the financial institution. Duties may be more generalized in smaller facilities and very specialized at larger institutions. The nature of the bank's business and the array of services it offers may also determine a clerk's duties. Services may differ somewhat in a commercial bank from those in a savings bank, trust company, credit union, or savings and loan. In the past, banks generally lent money to businesses, while savings and loan and credit unions lent to individuals, but these differences are slowly disappearing over time.

Collection clerks process checks, coupons, and drafts that customers present to the financial institution for special handling.

Commodity-loan clerks keep track of commodities (usually farm products) used as collateral by the foreign departments of large banks.

Banks employ *bookkeepers* to keep track of countless types of financial and administrative information. *Bookkeeping clerks* file checks, alphabetize paperwork to assist senior bookkeepers, and sort and list various other kinds of material.

Proof machine operators handle a machine that, in one single operation, can sort checks and other papers, add their amounts, and record totals. *Transit clerks* sort and list checks and drafts on other banks and prepare them for mailing back to those banks. *Statement clerks* send customers their account statements listing the withdrawals and deposits they have made. *Bookkeeping machine operators* maintain records of the various deposits, checks, and other items that are credited to or charged against customer accounts. Often they cancel checks and file them, provide customers with information about account balances, and prepare customers' statements for mailing.

Messengers deliver checks, drafts, letters, and other business papers to other financial institutions, business firms, and local and federal government agencies. Messengers who work only within the bank are often known as *pages. Trust-mail clerks* keep track of mail in trust departments.

Other clerks—*collateral-and-safekeeping clerks, reserves clerks,* and *interest clerks*—collect and record information about collateral, reserves, and interest rates and payments. *Letter-of-credit clerks* keep track of letters of credit for export and import purposes. *Wire-transfer clerks* operate machines that direct the transfer of funds from one account to another.

Many banks now use computers to perform the routine tasks that workers formerly did by hand. To operate these new machines, banks employ *computer operators, tabulating machine operators, microfilming machine operators,* and *electronic reader-sorter operators. Encoder operators* run machines that print information on checks and other papers in magnetic ink so that machines can read them. *Control clerks* keep track of all the data and paperwork transacted through the electronic data processing divisions.

In addition to working in banks, people employed by financial institutions may work at savings and loan associations, personal finance companies, credit unions, government agencies, and large businesses operating credit offices. Although tellers, clerks, and other workers' duties may differ among institutions, the needs for accuracy and honesty are the same. Financial institutions are usually pleasant, quiet places to work and have very up-to-date equipment and business machines. People who work in banking should be of good character and enjoy detailed work.

REQUIREMENTS

High School

Most banks today prefer to hire individuals who have completed high school. If you take courses in bookkeeping, mathematics, business arithmetic, and business machines while in high school, you may have an advantage when applying for a job. In addition, anyone working in a bank should be able to use computers, so be sure to take computer science courses. Take English, speech, and foreign language classes to improve your communication skills, which you will need when interacting with customers and other workers. Some banks are interested in hiring college graduates (or those who have completed at least two years of college training) who can eventually move into managerial positions. Exchange clerks may be expected to know foreign languages.

Postsecondary Training

Once hired, tellers, clerks, and related workers typically receive on-the-job training. At large institutions, tellers usually receive about one week of classroom training and then undergo on-the-job training for several weeks before they are allowed to work independently. Smaller financial institutions may only provide the on-the-job training in which new tellers are supervised in their work by experienced employees. Clerks may also need to undergo classroom instruction; for example, a bookkeeping clerk may need to take a class covering a certain computer program.

To enhance your possibility of getting a job as well as increase your skills, you may want to take business-related courses or courses for those in the financial industry at a local community college. Courses that may be helpful to take include records management, office systems and procedures, and computer database programming. Those with the most skills and training will find they usually have the best possibilities for advancing.

Numerous educational opportunities will be available to you once you have begun working—and gaining experience—in the financial world. For example, the educational division of the American Bankers Association—the American Institute of Banking—has a vast array of adult education classes in business fields and offers training courses in numerous parts of the country that enable people to earn standard or graduate certificates in bank training. Individuals may also enroll in correspondence study courses.

Bank tellers must be pleasant and courteous when assisting customers. *(Corbis)*

Other Requirements

Because the work involves many details, a prime requirement for all bank employees is accuracy. Even the slightest error can cause untold extra hours of work and inconvenience or even monetary loss. A pleasing and congenial personality and the ability to get along well with fellow workers and the public are also necessary in this employment.

The physical requirements of the work are not very demanding, although many of these workers spend much of the day standing, which can be tiring. While working in this field, you will be expected to be neat, clean, and appropriately dressed for business.

Banks occasionally require lie detector tests of applicants, as well as fingerprint and background investigations if the job requires handling currency and finances. Those employees handling money or having access to confidential financial information may have to qualify for a personal bond. Some banks now require pre-employment drug testing, and random testing for drugs while under employment is becoming more typical.

Although integrity and honesty are important traits for an employee in any type of work, they are absolutely necessary if you hope to be employed in banks and other financial institutions where large sums of money are handled every day. Workers must also exhibit sound judgment and intelligence in their job performance.

EXPLORING

You can explore the jobs in this field by visiting local financial institutions and talking with the directors of personnel or with people who work in these jobs. You should also consider serving as treasurer for your student government or a club that you are interested in. This will give you experience working with numbers and handling finances, as well as the opportunity to demonstrate responsibility. Learn about finances and the different kinds of financial instruments available by reading publications such as the business section of your local paper and *Money* magazine (also online at http://money.cnn.com).

Sometimes banks offer part-time employment to young people who feel they have a definite interest in pursuing a career in banking or those with business and clerical skills. Other types of part-time employment—where you learn basic business skills, how to interact with the public, and how to work well with other employees—may also be valuable training for those planning to enter these occupations.

EMPLOYERS

Approximately 499,000 workers are employed as tellers in the United States. Financial institution tellers, clerks, and related workers are employed by commercial banks and other depository institutions and by mortgage banks and other nondepository institutions.

STARTING OUT

Private and state employment agencies frequently list available positions for financial institution tellers, clerks, and related workers. Newspaper help-wanted advertisements carry listings for such employees. Some large financial institutions visit schools and colleges to recruit qualified applicants to fill positions on their staff.

If you are interested in a job as a financial institution teller or clerk, try contacting the director of personnel at a bank or other institution to see if any positions are available. If any jobs are open, you may be asked to come in and fill out an application. It is very important, however, to arrange the appointment first by telephone or mail because drop-in visits are disruptive and seldom welcome.

If you know someone who is willing to give you a personal introduction to the director of personnel or to the officers of a bank, you may find that this will help you secure employment. Personal and business references can be important to bank employers when they hire new personnel.

Many financial institution clerks begin their employment as trainees in certain types of work, such as business machine operation or general or specialized clerical duties. Employees may start out as file clerks, transit clerks, or bookkeeping clerks and in some cases as pages or messengers. In general, beginning jobs are determined by the size of the institution and the nature of its operations. In banking work, employees are sometimes trained in related job tasks so that they might be promoted later.

ADVANCEMENT

Many banks and financial institutions follow a "promote-from-within" policy. Promotions are usually given on the basis of past job performance and consider the employee's seniority, ability, and general personal qualities. Clerks who have done well and established good reputations may be promoted to teller positions. Tellers, in turn, may be promoted to head teller or supervisory positions such as department head. Some head tellers may be transferred from their main branch bank to a smaller branch bank where they have greater responsibilities.

Employees who show initiative in their jobs and pursue additional education may advance into low-level officer positions, such as assistant trust officer. The Bank Administration Institute and the American Institute of Banking (a division of the American Bankers Association) offer courses in various banking topics that can help employees learn new skills and prepare for promotions.

Advancement into the highest level positions typically require the employee to have a college or advanced degree.

EARNINGS

The earnings of financial institution workers vary by their specific duties, size and type of institution, and area of the country. According to the U.S. Department of Labor, full-time tellers earned a median annual income of about $19,830 in 2001. Salaries ranged from less than $15,000 to more than $26,610.

According to a salary guide by Robert Half International Inc., accounting clerks at large institutions had an annual salary range of $25,000 to $29,250 in 2000. At small institutions this range was from $22,250 to $26,250.

Financial institution tellers, clerks, and related workers may receive up to 12 paid holidays a year, depending on their locale. A two-week paid vacation is common after one year of service and can increase to three weeks after 10 or 15 years of service. Fringe benefits usually include group life and health insurance, hospitalization, and jointly financed retirement plans.

WORK ENVIRONMENT

Most financial institution workers work a 40-hour week. Tellers may need to work irregular hours or overtime, since many banks stay open until 8 P.M. on Fridays and are open Saturday mornings to accommodate their customers. Bank clerks and accounting department employees may have to work overtime at least once a week and often at the close of each month's banking operations to process important paperwork. Check-processing workers who are employed in large financial institutions may work late evening or night shifts. Those employees engaged in computer operations may also work evening or night shifts because this equipment is usually run around the clock. Pay for overtime work is usually straight compensation.

Banks and other depository institutions are usually air-conditioned, pleasantly decorated, and comfortably furnished. Financial institutions have excellent alarm systems and many built-in features that offer protection to workers and facilities. Although the work is not physically strenuous, tellers do have to spend much of their time on their feet. The work clerks and others perform is usually of a very repetitive nature, and the duties are very similar from day to day. Most of the work is paperwork, computer entry, data processing, and other mechanical processes. Clerks do not frequently have contact with customers or clients. Tellers, on the other hand, have extended contact with the public and must always remain polite, even under trying circumstances. Tellers, clerks, and others must be able to work closely with each other, sometimes on joint tasks, as well as under supervision.

OUTLOOK

Job outlooks, naturally, vary by position. The U.S. Department of Labor predicts a decline in employment of financial institution tellers over the next several years. Reasons for this projected decline include overexpansion by banks and competition from companies offering bank-like services. This has resulted in closings, mergers, and consolidations in the banking industry, meaning there are fewer employers in the field. Furthermore, the increasing use of automatic teller machines, banking by telephone and computer, and other technologies has resulted in either increased teller efficiency or removed the need for tellers altogether. Most employment opportunities for tellers will come from the need to replace those who have left the field.

Employment outlook for clerks and related workers, however, is slightly better, with little or no change expected over the next several years. Again, mergers, closings, and the use of computers and automated technologies contribute to containing the number of new positions available. Due to their repetitive natures, turnover in these jobs is high. Most job openings come from the need to find replacement workers for those who have left. In addition, financial institutions need to employ a large number of people to function properly.

It seems likely that the increasing use of computers and electronic data processing methods will only continue to curtail the numbers of workers needed for these positions. Nevertheless, because of the large size of these occupations, there should be many opportunities for replacement workers.

FOR MORE INFORMATION

The ABA has general information about the banking industry and information on education available through the American Institute of Banking.

American Bankers Association (ABA)
1120 Connecticut Avenue, NW
Washington, DC 20036
Tel: 800-226-5377
http://www.aba.com

The Bank Administration Institute (BAI) offers a number of online courses such as "Introduction to Checks" and "Cash Handling Techniques." For more education information, visit its website.

Bank Administration Institute (BAI)
One North Franklin, Suite 1000
Chicago, IL 60606-3421
Tel: 800-224-9889
Email: info@bai.org
http://www.bai.org

Hotel Desk Clerks

OVERVIEW

Hotel desk clerks work the front desk and are responsible for performing a variety of services, such as registering guests, assigning rooms, and providing general information. For many guests, the front desk worker gives them their first impression of the hotel. There are about 177,000 desk clerks employed at lodging properties, large and small, in the United States. Three out of 10 clerks work part time.

HISTORY

The very first desk clerks were simply the owners of a lodging establishment or members of their family. Besides managing the inn, cleaning the rooms, and cooking the food, the innkeepers were responsible for assigning rooms and collecting fees. As hotels grew bigger, many consolidated to create chains, such as the Statler Hotels or Holiday Inn. Sometimes a single owner was responsible for a number of properties. Innkeepers realized they needed help from employees apart from their immediate families. Desk clerks were trusted with managing the duties of the front desk—welcoming guests, assigning rooms, and maintaining hotel records.

Today, front office workers rely on computers to reduce paperwork, keep better records, and manage reservation systems. New software is constantly being developed to help the front office. For example, the Front Desk Resort Management System updates the master registry book by keeping track of reservations and guest information. Many guests now opt to use the in-room video express checkout instead of waiting in line. Even with such technological advancements, desk clerks are still

QUICK FACTS

School Subjects
Business
Computer science
Speech

Personal Skills
Following instructions
Helping/teaching

Work Environment
Primarily indoors
Primarily one location

Minimum Education Level
High school diploma

Salary Range
$12,690 to $16,920 to $23,300+

Certification or Licensing
Voluntary

Outlook
Faster than the average

DOT
238

GOE
07.04.03

NOC
6435

O*NET-SOC
43-4081.00

needed to staff the front desk. Guests like personal attention to certain details such as answering their questions and handling special requests. Even video checkouts are processed by desk clerks, who also then mail folios to guests.

THE JOB

The duties of the desk clerk, also known as *front office worker*, can be separated into four categories: process reservations, register the guest, serve as primary guest liaison, and process guest departure.

Process reservations. Desk clerks, or more specifically, *reservation clerks,* handle the duties of guest reservations, most often over the phone. They determine if the requested date is available, quote rates, record advance deposits or prepayments, confirm room reservations, and describe policies and services to guests. Reservation clerks, when dealing with reservation discrepancies, may have to retrieve hotel records or change or cancel the reservation to resolve the problem to the guest's satisfaction. Reservation clerks must also analyze the guest's special needs while at the hotel and relay them to the proper department.

Register the guest. After greeting the guest, desk clerks obtain and verify the required registration information, such as the guest's name, address, and length of stay. A credit card is usually required as a deposit or guarantee. Once the paperwork is done, room keys or key cards are issued, and guests are directed to their rooms.

Serve as primary guest liaison. Desk clerks often act as a buffer between the hotel and the guest. When guests have problems, have special requests, or encounter difficulties, they usually turn to the most visible person for help—the desk clerk. Some services provided to guests are laundry and valet requests, wake-up calls, and delivery of mail or messages. Clerks may also provide general information regarding the hotel or surrounding community. Their most important task, however, is to quickly address requests and complaints or to redirect the guest to the proper department.

Process guest departures. In some lodging establishments, a guest can choose to settle his or her account while in the room via the express, or video, checkout. Room charges are tallied on screen and charged to the customer's credit card. Desk clerks settle video checkouts at the end of the day and send folios to the guest's home address. However, many people still choose to personally check out at the front desk. After verifying and explaining all room charges, the desk clerk can begin to settle the guest's account. Sometimes, if credit authorization is declined, the clerk may have to politely negotiate an

After checking a couple into the hotel, a reservation clerk gives directions to a popular restaurant. *(Corbis)*

alternate method of payment. After thanking the guest and listening to any comments, positive or negative, the desk clerk can move on to the next customer or task.

Front office workers are responsible for keeping the hotel's information systems up to date. Many hotels now keep detailed information on their guests—such as the reason for their stay, their likes, and dislikes—and use this information for future marketing needs. Depending on the type or size of the hotel, they may also be responsible for working the switchboard, bookkeeping, house banks and petty cash, daily bank deposits, and recoding key cards. In addition, they must keep the front desk area clean and presentable.

REQUIREMENTS

High School
High school classes are a useful foundation for a career in the hotel industry. Concentrate on classes such as business, marketing, and even psychology to prepare yourself for this people-oriented job. Be sure to take English and speech courses to hone your communications skills. Lynda Witry, front desk supervisor at the Giorgios Hotel and Conference Center in Orland Park, Illinois, found her high school computer and typing classes helpful. "Being able to type—not the

hunt-and-peck method—makes working on the computer faster." According to Witry, it helps to know how to compute percentages and discounts, so don't forget your math!

Postsecondary Training
If you are hoping to use a desk clerk job as a stepping stone to a management position, you should seriously consider a degree in hotel management. College courses that will be helpful to your career include human relations, finance, and practical classes, such as hospitality supervision and front office procedures.

Internships are a great way to earn work experience, course credit, and most importantly, a chance to distinguish yourself from other applicants during an interview. Check with your high school guidance counselor or career center for a listing of available hospitality internships and schools that have two- or four-year programs, or contact the Educational Institute of the American Hotel and Lodging Association.

Certification or Licensing
Certification is not a requirement for the position of desk clerk, though it is considered by many as a measure of industry knowledge and experience. Programs, such as those offered by the Educational Institute of the American Hotel and Lodging Association, are designed to help improve job performance and advancement potential and keep you up-to-date on industry changes. The Registry program is specifically designed for desk clerks and other entry-level positions.

Other Requirements
"Desk clerks should be great communicators," says Witry. "They need to be able to deal with different kinds of people to be successful in this job." Organization, flexibility, and patience are some qualities needed when handling different situations and tasks simultaneously. You should be courteous and eager to help, even at times when the guests are demanding. When unable to help, you must be able to relay the guests' demands to the proper department. As a desk clerk, you will spend the majority of the day on your feet, so you should be in good physical condition. Computer knowledge, good phone manners, and readable penmanship are desirable for this job. Fluency in other languages, though not a requirement, is a great plus.

Good grooming habits are essential for this high visibility job. Strive for a professional look. Industry "don'ts" include unkempt or shocking hairstyles, excessive jewelry, and heavy or dramatic make-up. Desk clerks usually wear uniforms provided by the hotel that are cleaned free of charge at some hotels.

EXPLORING

The best way to explore this industry is to work in a hotel after school or during summer vacations. Although you may not land a desk clerk position, you may be hired as a waiter, waitress, dining-room attendant, or for a housekeeping position. You will be able to talk to people in the industry and learn the pros and cons of each job. If you can't find a job in the hotel industry, you might consider asking your guidance counselor to arrange an information interview with someone working in the field.

EMPLOYERS

Approximately 177,000 hotel, motel, and resort desk clerks are employed in the United States. Because hotels and motels are found worldwide, job opportunities for desk clerks are plentiful. The amount of responsibility given to a desk clerk depends on the size and type of lodging establishment. Larger hotels (usually located in busy urban areas), such as the 650-room Sheraton Manhattan in New York, may have separate departments, each responsible for answering phones, making advance reservations, or processing guest arrivals. The pace of work may be more frenzied at times because of the higher guest count. The Holiday Inn-Crown Plaza in Indianapolis, Indiana, a hotel on the small side, may have to combine departments to accommodate a smaller staff.

STARTING OUT

Many jobs are posted in newspaper want ads, trade magazines, or hotel employee newsletters. Hoteljobs.com (http://www.hoteljobs.com) is a website where you can post your resume and search for jobs nation-wide. High school job centers and their counselors are helpful in providing guidance, handbooks, and literature to interested students. They may even post part-time or seasonal work available in the field.

Hiring requirements vary from employer to employer, but most hotels look for candidates with work experience as well as education. Many desk clerks have a high school degree or the equivalent; but those ambitious enough to someday run the management track should consider obtaining an associate's or bachelor's degree in hotel management or a similar program. When applying for a job, experience in the hotel industry is a definite plus, although experience in the restaurant trade, customer service, or retail is equally valuable.

ADVANCEMENT

Desk clerks and reservation clerks are both considered entry-level positions. Promotions within the front office could lead to jobs as front desk supervisor or front office manager. Further advancement may be to the position of assistant hotel manager. It is also possible to move to other departments within the hotel, such as banquets or the sales department. Job promotions, especially to the management level, will be easier to obtain with further education.

EARNINGS

Salary.com reports that a typical front desk clerk earned a median base salary of $17,287 in 2002. Half of the people in this job earn between $14,085 and $21,215. According to the U.S. Department of Labor, median annual earnings of hotel, motel, and resort desk clerks were $16,920 in 2001. The lowest paid 10 percent of these workers earned $12,690 per year, while the highest-paid 10 percent made $23,300 annually. Salaries depend on the size, type, and location of the hotel.

After a probationary period, usually 90 days, the front office worker is frequently offered medical and sometimes dental insurance, vacation and sick days, paid holidays, and employee discounts. Many companies offer employees several free nights' stay per year at any of their properties.

WORK ENVIRONMENT

The front desk is located inside the hotel lobby, which is often clean and well decorated for the benefit of the guests. Desk clerks are on their feet most of the day, greeting guests and processing the paperwork needed for check-ins and check-outs. Most full-time desk clerks work a normal eight-hour day. However, because hotels are open 24 hours a day, it may be necessary for new employees with little seniority to work less-desirable shifts. Some holiday work should be expected.

This industry, as a rule, tends to have a high turnover rate. Larger hotels, especially those located in busy urban areas, may offer faster opportunities for advancement. Job openings are created as people climb the corporate ladder or leave the workforce for other reasons.

OUTLOOK

According to the *Occupational Outlook Handbook*, employment of hotel desk clerks is expected to grow faster than the average over the next several years. While hotel bookings have declined since the terrorist events of September 11, 2001, most industry experts believe the slowdown is temporary. The economic recession also has had an effect on both business and pleasure travel, although some recovery is expected within the next several years. These trends may affect employment of desk clerks, but people still need to travel for business and pleasure. Consequently, dependable desk clerks will be needed to work the front desk and reservation clerks will be needed to sell the rooms.

Jobs will be most plentiful with hotels located in busy urban areas, where there tend to be higher turnover rates. Larger hotels are known to pay higher wages, promote faster, and be more open to sending employees to further education classes and seminars. Downsides to working in a hotel in a big city include a high cost of living, which will probably eat up the pay difference that such a setting can provide. Also, employees of large-staffed hotels tend to experience less camaraderie among co-workers.

Most skills needed to be a good desk clerk are learned on the job. On-site training is a common method of continuing education, though hotels may choose to send their management-track employees to off-site seminars or continuing education classes.

FOR MORE INFORMATION

For career opportunities, certification, or educational information, contact:

American Hotel and Lodging Association
1201 New York Avenue, NW, Suite 600
Washington, DC 20005-3931
Tel: 202-289-3100
http://www.ahla.com

For information on scholarships, contact:

American Hotel and Lodging Foundation
1201 New York Avenue, NW, Suite 600
Washington, DC 20005-3931
Tel: 202-289-3180
Email: ahlef@ahlef.org
http://www.ahlf.org

For career information and development and training programs, contact:

Educational Institute of the American Hotel and Lodging Association
800 North Magnolia Avenue, Suite 1800
Orlando, FL 32803
Tel: 800-752-4567
http://www.ei-ahla.org

For a listing of schools with programs in hotel management, contact:

International Council on Hotel, Restaurant, and Institutional Education
2613 North Parham Road, 2nd Floor
Richmond, VA 23294
Tel: 804-346-4800
Email: info@chrie.org
http://chrie.org

Insurance Policy Processing Workers

OVERVIEW

Insurance policy processing workers perform a variety of clerical and administrative tasks that ensure that insurance applications and claims are handled in an efficient and timely manner. They review new applications, make adjustments to existing policies, work on policies that are to be reinstated, check the accuracy of company records, verify client information, and compile information used in claim settlements. Insurance policy processing personnel also handle business correspondence relating to any of the above duties. They use computers, word processors, calculators, and other office equipment in the course of their work. There are approximately 289,000 insurance policy processing workers employed in the United States.

HISTORY

Organized insurance was first developed in the shipping industry during the late 1600s as a means of sharing the risks of commercial voyages. Underwriters received a fee for the portion of the financial responsibility they covered.

As the need for further protection developed, other types of insurance were created. After the London Fire of 1666, fire insurance became available in England. Life insurance first appeared in the United States in 1759, accident insurance followed in 1863, and automobile insurance was instituted in 1898.

Now, millions of dollars worth of insurance policies are written every day. Skilled claims examiners, medical-voucher clerks, and

QUICK FACTS

School Subjects
Business
Computer science
Mathematics

Personal Skills
Following instructions
Leadership/management

Work Environment
Primarily indoors
Primarily one location

Minimum Education Level
High school diploma

Salary Range
$19,340 to $28,480 to
$45,410+

Certification or Licensing
None available

Outlook
Decline

DOT
219

GOE
07.01.04

NOC
1434

O*NET-SOC
13-1031.01, 43-9041.00,
43-9041.01, 43-9041.02

other insurance workers are needed to process applications and claims accurately and efficiently so clients get the coverage to which they are entitled.

THE JOB

Insurance policy processing workers are involved in all aspects of handling insurance applications and settling claims (or requests from policy owners regarding payment). The individual policies are sold by an *insurance agent* or *broker,* who sends the policies to processing workers and waits to see whether the company accepts the policy under the terms as written. The agent or the customer may contact policy-processing workers many times during the life of a policy for various services. *Claims examiners* review settled insurance claims to verify that payments have been made according to company procedures and are in line with the information provided in the claim form. These professionals may also need to contact policy processing clerks in the course of reviewing settlements. While a policy processing worker may be assigned a variety of tasks, insurance companies increasingly rely on specialists to perform specific functions.

Claims clerks review insurance claim forms for accuracy and completeness. Frequently, this involves calling or writing the insured party or other people involved to secure missing information. After placing this data in a claims file, the clerk reviews the insurance policy to determine the coverage. Routine claims are transmitted for payment; if further investigation is needed, the clerk informs the claims supervisor.

Claims supervisors not only direct the work of claims clerks but are also responsible for informing policy owners and beneficiaries of the procedures for filing claims. They submit claim liability statements for review by the actuarial department and inform department supervisors of the status of claims.

Reviewers check completed insurance applications to ensure that all questions have been answered by the applicants. They contact insurance agents to inform them of any problems with the applications; if they don't find any problems, reviewers suggest that policies be approved and delivered to applicants. Reviewers may collect premiums from new policy owners and provide management with updates on new business.

Policy-change clerks compile information on changes in insurance policies, such as a change in beneficiaries, and determine if the proposed changes conform to company policy and state law. Using rate books and a knowledge of specific types of policies, these clerks calculate new premiums and make appropriate adjustments to accounts. Policy-change clerks may help write a new policy with the client's specified changes or prepare a rider to an existing policy.

Cancellation clerks cancel insurance policies as directed by insurance agents. They compute any refund due and mail any appropriate refund and the cancellation notice to the policy owner. Clerks also notify the bookkeeping department of the cancellation and send a notice to the insurance agent.

Revival clerks approve reinstatement of customers' insurance policies if the reason for the lapse in service, such as an overdue premium, is corrected within a specified time limit. They compare answers given by the policy owner on the reinstatement application with those previously approved by the company, and they examine company records to see if there are any circumstances that make reinstatement impossible. Revival clerks calculate the irregular premium and the reinstatement penalty due when the reinstatement is approved, type notices of company action (approval or denial of reinstatement), and send this notification to the policy owner.

Insurance checkers verify the accuracy and completeness of insurance company records by comparing the computations on premiums paid and dividends due on individual forms. They then check that information against similar information on other applications. They also verify personal information on applications, such as the name, age, address, and value of property of the policy owner, and they proofread all material concerning insurance coverage before it is sent to policy owners.

Insurance agents must apply to insurance companies in order to represent the companies and sell their policies. *Agent-contract clerks* evaluate the ability and character of prospective insurance agents and approve or reject their contracts to sell insurance for a company. They review the prospective agent's application for relevant work experience and other qualifications and check the applicant's personal references to see if they meet company standards. Agent-contract clerks correspond with both the prospective agent and company officials to explain their decision to accept or reject individual applications.

Medical-voucher clerks analyze vouchers sent by doctors who have completed medical examinations of insurance applicants and approve payment of these vouchers based on standard rates. These clerks note the doctor's fee on a form and forward the form and the voucher to the insurance company's bookkeeper or other appropriate personnel for further approval and payment.

Insurance Facts

- Each year, 98,000 Americans die as a result of medical malpractice.

- The Terrorism Risk Insurance Act of 2002 is a federal law that requires all insurers to make available terrorism coverage to commercial risks.

- According to the Insurance Information Institute, the cost of insuring homes is expected to rise by nine percent in 2003.

REQUIREMENTS

High School

A high school diploma is usually sufficient for beginning insurance policy processing workers. To prepare yourself for this job, you should take courses in English, mathematics, and computer science while in high school. In addition, take as many business-related courses as possible, such as typing, word processing, and bookkeeping.

Postsecondary Training

Community colleges and vocational schools often offer business education courses that provide training for insurance policy processing workers. You may want to consider taking these courses to improve your possibilities for advancement to supervisory positions.

Other Requirements

In order to succeed in this field, you should have some aptitude with business machines, the ability to concentrate for long periods of time on repetitive tasks, and mathematical skills. Legible handwriting is a necessity. Because you will often work with policy owners and other workers, you must be able to communicate effectively and work well with others. In addition, insurance policy processing workers need to be familiar with state and federal insurance laws and regulations. They should find systematic and orderly work appealing, and they should like to work on detailed tasks.

Other personal qualifications include dependability, trustworthiness, and a neat personal appearance. Insurance policy processing personnel who work for the federal government may need to pass a civil service examination.

EXPLORING

You can get experience in this field by assuming clerical or bookkeeping responsibilities for a school club or other organization. In addition, some school work-study programs may have opportunities with insurance companies for part-time, on-the-job training. You might also get a part-time or summer job with an insurance company.

You can get training in office procedures and the operation of business machinery and computers through evening courses offered by business schools. Another way to gain insight into the responsibilities of insurance policy processing workers is to talk to someone already working in the field.

EMPLOYERS

Approximately 289,000 insurance claims and policy processing clerks are employed in the United States. Insurance companies are the principal employers of insurance policy processing workers. These workers may perform similar duties for real estate firms and the government.

STARTING OUT

If you are interested in securing an entry-level position, you should contact insurance agencies directly. Jobs may also be located through help-wanted advertisements or by using the local office of the U.S. Employment Service.

Some insurance companies may give you an aptitude test to determine your ability to work quickly and accurately. Work assignments may be made on the basis of the results of this test.

ADVANCEMENT

Many inexperienced workers begin as file clerks and advance to positions in policy processing. Insurance policy processing workers usually begin their employment handling the more routine tasks, such as reviewing insurance applications to ensure that all the questions have been answered. With experience, they may advance to more complicated tasks and assume a greater responsibility for complete assignments. Those who show the desire and ability may be promoted to clerical supervisory positions, with a corresponding increase in pay and work responsibilities. To become a claims adjuster or an underwriter, it is usually necessary to have a college degree or have taken specialized courses in insurance. Many such courses are available from local business or vocational colleges and various industry trade groups.

The high turnover rate among insurance policy processing workers increases opportunities for promotions. The number and kind of opportunities, however, may depend on the place of employment and the ability, training, and experience of the employee.

EARNINGS

Insurance policy processing workers' salaries varied depending on such factors as the worker's experience and the size and location of the employer. Generally, those working for large companies in big cities earned higher salaries. According to the U.S. Department of Labor, the median yearly income for insurance policy processing clerks was $28,480 in 2001. Salaries ranged from $19,340 to $45,410.

As full-time employees of insurance companies, policy processing workers usually receive the standard fringe benefits of vacation and sick pay, health insurance, and retirement plans.

WORK ENVIRONMENT

As is the case with most office workers, insurance policy processing employees work an average of 37–40 hours a week. Although the work environment is usually well ventilated and lighted, the job itself can be fairly routine and repetitive, with most of the work taking place at a desk. Policy processing workers often interact with other insurance professionals and policyholders, and they may work under close supervision.

Because many insurance companies offer 24-hour claims service to their policyholders, some claims clerks may work evenings and weekends. Many insurance workers are employed part-time or on a temporary basis.

OUTLOOK

The U.S. Department of Labor predicts that employment for insurance processing workers will decline over the next several years. This decline will be due to the increased use of data processing machines and other types of automated equipment that increase worker productivity and result in the need for fewer workers.

Many jobs will result from workers retiring or otherwise leaving the field. Employment opportunities should be best in and around large metropolitan areas, where the majority of large insurance companies are located. There should be an increase in the number of opportunities for temporary or part-time work, especially during busy business periods.

FOR MORE INFORMATION

For information on educational programs, contact:

Insurance Institute of America
720 Providence Road
PO Box 3016
Malvern, PA 19355-0716
Tel: 800-644-2101
Email: cserv@cpcuiia.org
http://www.aicpcu.org

Insurance Institute of Canada
18 King Street East, 6th Floor
Toronto, ON M5C 1C4, Canada
Tel: 416-362-8586
Email: genmail@iic-iac.org
http://www.iic-iac.org

Legal Secretaries

QUICK FACTS

School Subjects
English
Government
Journalism

Personal Skills
Communication/ideas
Following instructions

Work Environment
Primarily indoors
Primarily one location

Minimum Education Level
Some postsecondary training

Salary Range
$22,360 to $34,610 to
$53,280+

Certification or Licensing
Recommended

Outlook
About as fast as the average

DOT
201

GOE
07.01.03

NOC
1242

O*NET-SOC
43-6012.00

OVERVIEW

Legal secretaries, sometimes called *litigation secretaries* or *trial secretaries*, assist lawyers by performing the administrative and clerical duties in a law office or firm. Legal secretaries spend most of their time writing legal correspondence, preparing legal documents, performing research, and answering incoming calls and emails. Legal secretaries read and review many law journals to check for any new court decisions that may be important for cases pending at that time. Legal secretaries also maintain files and records, take notes during meetings or hearings, and assume all other general secretarial duties. Approximately 279,000 legal secretaries work in law offices and firms in the United States today.

HISTORY

Over the years, the law has become increasingly complex. In addition, increased litigation has led to a greater demand for lawyers to, first, explain the law, and second, to pursue its defense. Originally, lawyers hired secretaries for their small, one- or two-lawyer office to assist with general clerical duties. Typing letters, filing documents, and receiving clients were the main duties of these general secretaries. As lawyers were forced to spend more of their time dealing with the difficulties of the law and with their increased number of clientele, secretaries were given more responsibility. The secretaries were transformed from being mainly receptionists to managing the law office, at least the administrative side of it. Lawyers started to look to their secretaries more as legal assistants than receptionists.

Today legal secretaries are indispensable to most lawyers and play a major role in each client's case by streamlining all documentation, communication, and research into a usable source of information.

The legal secretary field has also grown in this computer age. "As an example of how information technology has transformed the profession, 20 years ago the rule was 'one lawyer, one secretary,'" says professional legal secretary Alexis Montgomery. "Now with computer word processing, specialized programs for legal practices, and information technology in all of its forms, typically one experienced legal secretary can handle two lawyers." Although most computer advances have helped the legal secretary field expand, some lawyers are using this technology to increase their own productivity. The lawyer can reassume some duties that the legal secretary does now—reducing the need for secretaries.

Although lawyers may be more computer-savvy, legal secretaries still play an important, but changing, role in law offices. For example, whereas before the legal secretary took dictation, typed out a letter, and then proofread it for accuracy, now the lawyer may type his own letter on the computer and ask the legal secretary to edit it and to fact check some of the main points. Lawyers aren't the only ones taking advantage of new technology; legal secretaries now have the advantage of using personal computers instead of electronic typewriters, and fax machines instead of telex machines. The World Wide Web has made research much easier as well.

THE JOB

Legal secretaries must be able to handle all the duties of a general secretary plus all the specific responsibilities that come with working for a lawyer. Although every law office or firm may vary in the exact duties required for the position, in general, most legal secretaries spend their time managing information that comes in and goes out of the law office. According to Alexis Montgomery, a typical day as a legal secretary begins with setting priorities. "Each day begins with reviewing the work to be done, which requires reading snail mail, email, and faxes to see how they might affect the day's priorities." Next, she says, the work is addressed according to priority. Work can include any number of things ranging from attending legal meetings to filling out trial and courtroom requests.

Legal secretaries may type letters and legal documents, such as subpoenas, appeals, and motions; handle incoming and outgoing mail; maintain a detailed filing system; and deliver legal documents to the court. Besides these duties, legal secretaries spend much of their time making appointments with clients, and dealing with client questions. "An important part of being an effective legal secretary is fielding telephone calls and all client contact efficiently and courteously," says Montgomery. "Often the client's primary contact is with the legal secretary and client satisfaction depends heavily on how helpful and courteous that contact is perceived." The legal secretary is a sort of personal assistant to one or more lawyers as well, and must maintain the calendars and schedules for the office. "Always knowing where your attorney can be found or whether another attorney can assist the client is an important part of the process," says Montgomery.

Legal secretaries are also called upon to conduct research for the cases that are current within the office. They may research and write legal briefs on a topic or case that is relevant to the lawyer's current cases. According to Rebecca Garland, legal advocate, research often takes up an entire day. "You may spend one whole day working on a legal brief for one client, and then spend the next day working on small things for several different cases." (Garland was trained as a legal secretary but is now using those skills to assist victims of domestic violence in obtaining personal protection orders.) Legal secretaries spend many hours researching cases in law libraries, public libraries, and on the Internet. Part of this research includes scouring legal journals and magazines looking for relevant laws and courtroom decisions that may affect the clientele.

Legal secretaries are also record-keepers. They help lawyers find information such as employment, medical, and criminal records. They also keep records from all previous clients and court cases for future use. Legal secretaries must also track and use various forms, such as trial request, client application, and accident report forms. "The bottom line is that legal secretaries process the paperwork generated by their attorneys," says Alexis Montgomery.

REQUIREMENTS

High School
Because a legal secretary must be able to communicate the attorney's ideas in written and oral form, it's important to get a firm grounding in English (especially writing), spelling, typing, and public speaking. Computers are used in most law offices, so be sure to gain computer experience while in high school. Government and political science courses will lay a foundation for legal knowledge. Classes that involve research are also important. Rebecca Garland says, "Learning

how to do research in the school or community library will go a long way in learning how to do research in a law library."

Postsecondary Training
Many legal secretaries receive training through established one- or two-year legal secretary programs. These programs are available at most business, vocational, and junior colleges. You could also obtain a four-year degree to get a more well-rounded education. Courses taken should focus on specific skills and knowledge needed by a legal secretary, such as personal computers, keyboarding, English, legal writing, editing, researching, and communication. The National Association of Legal Secretaries also offers a basic legal secretary training course. (See their contact information at the end of this article.)

As businesses continue to expand worldwide, employers are increasingly looking for candidates with bachelor's degrees and professional certifications.

Certification or Licensing
Two general legal secretary certifications are offered by the National Association of Legal Secretaries. After some preliminary office training, you can take an examination to receive the Accredited Legal Secretary (ALS) designation. This certification is for legal secretaries with education, but little to no experience. The exam has three parts and takes four hours to complete. Legal secretaries with three years of experience can become certified as a Professional Legal Secretary (PLS). The PLS certification designates a legal secretary with exceptional skills and experience. This exam has four parts and takes a full day to complete.

Other specific legal secretary certifications are given by Legal Secretaries International, Inc. You can become board certified in civil trial, probate, real estate, business law, or criminal law. Exams consist of three parts and take four hours to complete.

Other Requirements
To be employed as a legal secretary, you must learn a great deal of legal terminology and court structures and practices. Whether through study or experience, you must be able to grasp the inner workings of the law. You must also be able to learn computer programs quickly, especially word processing and database programs, and be able to use them skillfully. The ability to prioritize and balance different tasks is also necessary for the job. Legal secretaries must be organized and focused to handle their varying responsibilities.

EXPLORING

If this career interests you, suggest a career day at your school (if one isn't already scheduled) where professionals from a variety of careers give presentations. Be sure to let your career counselor know that you would like to have a legal secretary come as a guest speaker. Or you can ask your political science or government teacher to take your class on a field trip to a law library. Many law offices hire "runners" to deliver and file documents. Check with local law offices and offer your services for the summer or after school. You may also find it helpful to contact a local law firm and ask the legal secretary there if you can conduct an information interview.

EMPLOYERS

Approximately 279,00 legal secretaries are employed in the United States. The majority of legal secretaries work for law offices or law firms. Some government agencies on the state and national level also employ legal secretaries. More law firms and offices are located in Washington, D.C. and in larger metropolitan areas, so these regions offer more opportunities. However, most law offices and firms are now online. The Internet enables workers to send information easily from the law office to the courtroom, so offices are not forced to be located close to the courts. Legal secretaries are in demand anywhere lawyers practice.

STARTING OUT

Many legal secretaries get their first job through the career placement offices of their college or vocational school. Still other legal secretaries start by working part-time, gaining experience toward a first full-time position. Alexis Montgomery started out that way: "My first employment was as a staff secretary on a newspaper. Thereafter I worked as a 'floater' in a medium-sized law firm. [A *floater* is a secretary who is not assigned to any particular lawyer, but fills in for absent secretaries and handles overflow.] This job was my first exposure to the field and provided on-the-job training as a legal secretary." Montgomery also adds that working as a floater exposes you to a wide variety of legal practices—useful when deciding which area you want to specialize in. Don't forget to contact the local law offices in your area and let them know you are available; often direct contact now can lead to a job later.

ADVANCEMENT

Experienced legal secretaries are often promoted to oversee less experienced legal secretaries. Some firms have senior legal secretaries who are given more responsibility and less supervision duties. "In many cases more experienced legal secretaries do the drafting of letters and documents and pass them on to the attorney for revision or signature," says Montgomery. "As one becomes more experienced and proficient, the work of a legal secretary tends to blend into what is regarded as paralegal work." Legal secretaries may continue their education and become paralegals themselves. Many of the skills legal secretaries obtain can be transferred to almost any other office setting.

EARNINGS

According to the U.S. Department of Labor, the average salary for legal secretaries was approximately $34,610 in 2001. Starting salaries were $22,360; however, those with experience averaged much higher pay, earning more than $53,280. An attorney's rank in the firm will also affect the salary of his or her legal secretary; secretaries who work for a partner will earn higher salaries than those who work for an associate. Certified legal secretaries generally receive higher pay.

Most law firms provide employees with sick days, vacation days, and holidays. Health insurance, 401-K programs, and profit sharing may be offered as well. Some law firms offer in-house training or pay for off-site classes to increase their secretarial skills.

WORK ENVIRONMENT

Legal secretaries spend the majority of their day behind their desk at a computer. They spend lengthy periods of time typing or writing, which may cause hand and wrist strain. Long hours staring at a computer monitor may also cause eyestrain. Legal secretaries work with lawyers, other legal secretaries, clients, court personnel, library personnel, and other support workers. Some legal secretaries are supervised by senior legal secretaries; others are left largely unsupervised. Most legal secretaries are full-time employees who work a 40-hour week. Some are part-time workers who move into full-time status as they gain more experience. Because the legal secretary's work revolves around the lawyer, many secretaries work long hours of overtime. Montgomery comments, "It is the nature of litigation; often overtime and weekend work is necessary to meet the deadlines that pop up no matter how carefully one tries to anticipate them."

OUTLOOK

Because the legal services industry as a whole is growing, legal secretaries will be in demand. An increased need for lawyers in such areas as intellectual property cases will leave lawyers in need of assistance with their caseloads. Qualified legal secretaries will have plentiful job opportunities, especially in the larger metropolitan areas.

Technological advances in recent years have revolutionized traditional secretarial tasks such as typing or keeping correspondence. The use of email, scanners, and the Internet will make secretaries more productive in coming years. The downside to these advancements is a possible decrease in demand: fewer workers are needed to do the same workload. For the legal profession, however, advances in technology have only expanded the responsibilities for secretaries. According to the *Occupational Outlook Handbook*, employment for legal secretaries will continue to grow about as fast as the average for all occupations over the next several years.

FOR MORE INFORMATION

For information about certification and an online application form, contact:

Legal Secretaries International, Inc.
15 Greenway Drive
RR 4, Box 4225
Trinity, TX 75862-9324
Tel: 936-594-9234
http://www.legalsecretaries.org

For information on certification, job openings, and more, contact:
National Association of Legal Secretaries
314 East 3rd Street, Suite 210
Tulsa, OK 74120
Tel: 918-582-5188
Email: info@nals.org
http://www.nals.org

INTERVIEW

Edwina Klemm is the President of Legal Secretaries International, Inc. and has been a Certified Professional Legal Secretary since 1978. She has worked in Ohio, Texas, and Alaska in many areas of legal

practice, including appellate, insurance defense, construction litiga-
tion, plaintiff's litigation, corporate, natural resources, tax and estate
planning, domestic relations and adoption, and bankruptcy. She is
now Executive Secretary to the CEO of a Houston, Texas holding
company. Klemm spoke with the editors of Careers in Focus: Clerks
& Administrative Workers *about her career and the legal secretarial*
field in general.

Q. Please briefly describe your primary and secondary job duties.

A. I don't believe duties can be described as "primary" or "secondary." A legal secretary is there to support the attorneys with whom she or he works. Those duties depend on the size and type of office.

There is no brief description of duties and responsibilities in a law office. Depending on the size of the office, a secretary can expect heavy contact with court personnel, attorneys, and clients by phone and in the office. Other duties can include drafting documents and correspondence; finalizing documents for filing with the courts; posting attorney time and doing monthly billings; maintaining records on accounts payable and accounts receivable; copying and filing documents with the courts; copying and delivering documents to clients; supervision of law clerks and office clerks; maintenance of client files—indexing, tabbing, filing pleadings and correspondence; quarterly closing of files and removal to off-site storage or destruction according to office policy and a preset time table; dealing with office supply and other sales reps; maintaining office supplies; indexing discovery and other documents and maintaining a log of those documents for easy retrieval.

Generally, however, the secretary handles dictation, drafts correspondence and pleadings, begins preparation of shell documents for responses, and handles calls from clients, other attorneys and their staff, or the courts. Calendaring/docketing, filing, document organization, control of client documents, and case discovery may also be part of the job, again depending on the size of the office.

While most firms have a prohibition against secretaries being asked to handle an attorney's personal matters, some do end up reminding them of birthdays and anniversaries, keeping track of addresses and phone numbers, and maintaining some personal files.

Maintaining confidentiality is a very important part of the job. Secretaries are held to the same ethical requirements as attorneys and must maintain client and attorney privileges just as rigorously. Although a secretary cannot be disbarred or disciplined the way an attorney can, responsibility for missteps in this area falls to the supervising attorney and the firm. It behooves a secretary to know the ethical rules and adhere to them.

In my particular situation, I handle all the communications (written, telephonic, and electronic) for my employer. If he is not available for a call, most often the next person the caller requests is me. I also respond to his email, from dictation, handwritten notes, or general instruction for drafting a response. I handle all travel arrangements, and we don't use a travel agent. I work closely with our board of directors, responding to inquiries and providing information they may need. Because we are a company in growth mode, I also do research on potential areas of investment and provide reports as necessary.

Legal secretaries may go to the courthouse to file documents, but that is not typically part of their daily routine (unless they are in a small office or do not have courier service). They ought to know where the courthouse is and how to file a document, however, just in case (and that includes how many copies are needed for the filing).

In the past, I have accompanied my attorney to the hospital for will signings or for adoption matters. In one case, I went with him to pick up a baby being adopted by our clients. I've also gone out with process servers on assignment, attempting to serve documents, but that is not usually a job the legal secretary handles. I've also been called on to testify in several court proceedings.

Q. How did you train for this job?

A. Upon graduation from high school in San Antonio, I attended a six-week legal secretary training course at San Antonio College offered by Texas Employment under the Manpower Development and Training Act. At that time, Texas Employment gave employment tests to all graduating high school seniors. Only those with certain scores who did not indicate they were attending college were offered specialized training—medical or legal secretary. Since the medical secretary course was filled, I took the legal secretary training course. I've never had cause to regret it.

Q. How/where did you get your first job in this field? What did you do?

A. My first job as a legal secretary came about after completion of the training course I mentioned above. Texas Employment took our scores and recommendation by the instructor (a former legal secretary) and assigned us numbers. The list was sent to law offices and attorneys in San Antonio, and they set up interviews based on our "identifying number." My first job was with a small firm (father and two sons). I took dictation, prepared documents and correspondence, and did filing.

Q. What kind of sources were—and are—available to someone looking to get into this field? Newspaper classifieds? Word-of-mouth? Job search agencies? The Internet?

A. While all these sources are available, getting into the legal secretarial field requires some experience. Most firms are looking for someone with at least minimal legal experience. Some will hire a person with good secretarial skills and some work experience, but generally those are entry-level positions.

Q. What are the most important personal and professional qualities for people in your career?

A. Not everyone is capable of being a secretary, where one must be multi-talented, able to multi-task, with technical, human relations, and organizational skills. The following skills are also essential to being a good legal secretary: great people skills; ability to work under stressful conditions; attention to detail; ability to handle numerous tasks at one time; good writing skills; an excellent working knowledge of grammar, spelling, and punctuation; knowledge of local courts, rules, and procedures; ability to type documents and know what they mean; good proofreading ability, able to read for content as well as typographical errors; knowledge of how to format documents appropriately (i.e., court pleadings, appeal briefs, commercial documents, etc.); working knowledge of terminology and citation forms; an ability to take notes quickly (shorthand, speed writing, etc.) is a plus.

Q. What are some of the pros and cons of your job?

A. Pros: I've always been able to work and support myself without relying on anyone to help me.... I've had an opportunity to travel and meet new people in my profession through work with my professional association.

I've been able to develop writing and public speaking skills. I've had an opportunity to meet and work with some of the most powerful attorneys in the country, to meet celebrity clients, and attend celebrity social functions. Being a legal secretary has also enabled me to grow personally. For all the bad press lawyers get (some of it rightly deserved), working in the legal field gives you an insight into the processes that make this country run.

Cons: If you hate dealing with people with problems, hate working with tight deadlines, or hate the idea of not being the boss, this is definitely not the career field for you. If you are not detail-oriented, you may want to reconsider your career choice. …Failure to pay attention to details can cause problems at some future date, and one thing attorneys hate is having something come back to bite them.

Q. What is the most important piece of advice that you have to offer students as they graduate and look for jobs in this field?

A. Find a mentor. One of the best ways to learn in this field (any field, actually) is to have a mentor who is willing to answer your questions and help you learn and grow in your career field. Join a professional association for personal and career growth; membership in a professional association, where networking and education are available, is one of the best ways to achieve potential. It's also a good way to find a mentor.

Q. What is the future employment outlook for your career?

A. I believe there will always be a need for legal secretaries. Even with speech-recognition programs that enable computers to type from the spoken word, legal secretaries will always be needed to oversee the daily work of the law office—the phone calls, calendaring, filing, daily correspondence, transcription, etc. In many offices, the legal secretary serves as legal assistant or paralegal, office manager, bookkeeper, den mother, personal assistant, and conscience. In others, she serves as the attorney's personal assistant and supervisor of tasks, keeping track of assignments delegated to legal assistants or paralegals and helping the attorney(s) juggle the caseload to ensure that each client receives the highest quality legal services.

No matter what we may be called in the future, legal secretaries will always be able to find a job. After all, it was legal secretaries who met the challenge to do more than answer the phone and type, pioneering the way for paralegal and legal assistant job classifications.

Library Technicians

OVERVIEW

Library technicians, sometimes called *library technical assistants,* work in all areas of library services, supporting professional librarians or working independently to help people access information. They order and catalog books; help library patrons locate materials; and make the library's services and facilities readily available. Technicians verify bibliographic information on orders, and perform basic cataloging of materials received. They answer routine questions about library services and refer questions requiring professional help to librarians. Technicians also help with circulation desk operations and oversee the work of stack workers and catalog-card typists. They circulate audiovisual equipment and materials and inspect items upon return. Approximately 109,000 library technicians are employed in the United States.

HISTORY

The earliest libraries, referred to in Egyptian manuscripts, date from 3000 B.C. The centuries since have seen great changes in libraries and their place in society. In the Middle Ages, books were so rare that they were often chained to shelves to prevent loss. The inventions of the printing press and movable type increased the literacy rate, and the increasing availability of books and periodicals all contributed to the growth of libraries.

The growth of public education in the 1800s was accompanied by a rapid growth of public libraries across the United States, greatly aided in the latter part of the century by the generosity of philanthropists such as Andrew Carnegie. Aids to locating information

QUICK FACTS

School Subjects
Computer science
English

Personal Skills
Helping/teaching
Technical/scientific

Work Environment
Primarily indoors
Primarily one location

Minimum Education Level
Associate's degree

Salary Range
$14,190 to $23,790 to
$37,420+

Certification or Licensing
None available

Outlook
About as fast as the average

DOT
100

GOE
11.02.04

NOC
5211

O*NET-SOC
25-4031.00

The Library of Congress

The Library of Congress in Washington, D.C. is considered the nation's library. It was created in 1800 when the site of the U.S. capital moved from Philadelphia to Washington, D.C. At the time it was established, the Library had only 740 books and three maps in its collection. Now, it hosts the largest and most diverse collection of knowledge and creativity in recorded history, comprising 18 million books, 2.5 million recordings, 12 million photographs, 4.5 million maps, and 54 million manuscripts. The Library of Congress celebrated its 200th birthday in 2000.

Source: Library of Congress (http://www.loc.gov)

were developed, such as the Dewey Decimal System in 1876 and Poole's Index to Periodical Literature in 1882, and these aids made libraries much more convenient for users. The American Library Association was founded in 1876, an event that is usually regarded as marking the birth of librarianship as a profession.

The great increase in the amount of recorded information in the 20th century has led to a steady increase in the number of library facilities and services. It is estimated that the amount of information published on almost every general subject doubles every 10–20 years. Libraries depend on trained personnel to keep informed about what new information is available, to be selective about what materials are purchased, and to share materials with other libraries as an extension of their own resources.

As the responsibilities of librarians became more complex, the need for technically trained workers to support them became evident. During the 1940s many libraries began training their own support staffs. In-service training programs proved costly, however, and since 1965 the bulk of library technician training has been assumed by community colleges. Now that computers are used for many of the technical and user services, library technicians perform many of the tasks once handled exclusively by librarians.

THE JOB

Work in libraries falls into three general categories: technical services, user services, and administrative services. Library technicians may be involved with the responsibilities of any of these areas.

In technical services, library technicians are involved with acquiring resources and then organizing them so the material can be easily accessed. They process order requests, verify bibliographic information, and prepare order forms for new materials, such as books, magazines, journals, videos, and CD-ROMs. They perform routine cataloging of new materials and record information about the new materials in computer files or on cards to be stored in catalog drawers. The *acquisitions technicians, classifiers,* and *catalogers* who perform these functions make information available for the library users. Technicians who work for interlibrary loan departments may arrange for one library to borrow materials from another library or for a library to temporarily display a special collection. They might make basic repairs to damaged books or refer the materials to a preservation department for more comprehensive conservation. A *circulation counter attendant* helps readers check out materials and collects late fines for overdue books. *Media technicians* operate audiovisual equipment for library media programs and maintain the equipment in working order. They often prepare graphic artwork and television programs.

Under the guidance of librarians in user services, technicians work directly with library patrons and help them to access the information needed for their research. They direct library patrons to the computer or card catalog in response to inquiries and assist with identifying the library's holdings. They describe the general arrangement of the library for new patrons and answer basic questions about the library's collections. They may also help patrons use microfiche and microfilm equipment. They may help them locate materials in an interlibrary system's computerized listing of holdings. *Reference library technicians* specialize in locating and researching information. *Children's library technicians* and *young-adult library technicians* specialize in getting children and young adults interested in books, reading, and learning by sponsoring summer reading programs, reading hours, puppet shows, literacy contests, and other fun activities.

Technicians who work in administrative services help with the management of the library. They might help prepare budgets, coordinate the efforts of different departments within the library, write policy and procedures, and work to develop the library's collection. If they have more responsibility they might supervise and coordinate staff members, recruit and supervise volunteers, organize fund-raising efforts, sit on community boards, and develop programs to promote and encourage reading and learning in the community.

The particular responsibilities of a library technician vary according to the type of library. *Academic library technicians* work in university or college libraries, assisting professors and students in their research needs. Their work would revolve around handling reference materials and specialized journals. *School library technicians* work with *school library media specialists,* assisting teachers and students in utilizing the print and nonprint resources of a school library media center.

Library technicians also work in special libraries maintained by government agencies, corporations, law firms, advertising agencies, museums, professional associations, medical centers, religious organizations, and research laboratories. Library technicians in special libraries deal with information tailored to the specific needs and interests of the particular organization. They may also organize bibliographies, prepare abstracts and indexes of current periodicals, or research and analyze information on particular issues.

Library technicians develop and index computerized databases to organize information collected in the library. They also help library patrons use computers to access the information stored in their own databases or in remote databases. With the increasing use of automated information systems, many libraries hire *automated system technicians* to help plan and operate computer systems and *information technicians* to help design and develop information storage retrieval systems and procedures for collecting, organizing, interpreting, and classifying information.

In the past, library technicians functioned solely as the librarian's support staff, but this situation has evolved over the years. Library technicians continue to refer questions or problems requiring professional experience and judgment to librarians. However, with the increasing use of computer systems in libraries, library technicians now perform many of the technical and user service responsibilities once performed by librarians, thereby freeing librarians to focus more on acquisitions and administrative responsibilities. In some cases a library technician may handle the same responsibilities as a librarian, even in place of a librarian.

REQUIREMENTS

High School
If you are considering a career as a library technician, you should take a college preparatory course load. Classes in English, history, literature, foreign languages, computers, and mathematics are crucial to giving you a strong background in the skills you will need as a library technician. Strong verbal and writing skills are especially important, so take all the classes you can to help you develop facility in speaking and writing. Any special knowledge of a particular subject mat-

ter can also be beneficial. For instance, if you have a strong interest in geography, you may want to consider pursuing a technical assistant position in a map room of a library.

Postsecondary Training
The technical nature of the work performed by library technicians, especially when working in technical services, is prompting more and more libraries to hire only high school graduates who have gone on to complete a two-year program in library technology. Many enroll in a two-year certificate program that, upon graduation, bestows the title Library Technical Assistant (LTA). Typical programs include courses in the basic purpose and functions of libraries; technical courses in processing materials, cataloging acquisitions, library services, and use of the Internet; and one year of liberal arts studies. Persons entering such programs should understand that the library-related courses they take will not apply toward a professional degree in library science.

For some positions, a bachelor's degree may be required in a specific area, such as art history for work in a museum library, or sociology for a position at YMCA library. Specialized study in a foreign language may be helpful, since most libraries have materials in many languages, and all of those materials must be cataloged and processed for library patrons to use. Also, not all library users speak English; a library employee who is able to communicate with all users in person, on the telephone, and in writing is especially effective. While in college, you will probably be required to take courses in the liberal arts, such as sociology, psychology, speech, history, and literature, among others.

Some smaller libraries, especially in rural communities, may hire persons with only a high school education for library technician positions. Some libraries may hire individuals who have prior work experience, and some may provide their own training for inexperienced individuals. On the other hand, some libraries may only hire library technicians who have earned associate's or bachelor's degrees.

Other Requirements
Whatever your educational or training background, you should demonstrate aptitude for careful, detailed, analytical work. You should enjoy problem solving and working with people as well as with books and other library materials. Good interpersonal skills are invaluable, since library technicians often have much public contact. As a library technician, you should possess patience and flexibility and should not mind being interrupted frequently to answer questions from library patrons.

You should also exhibit good judgment; you'll need to know when you are able to assist a user, and when the problem must be referred to a professional librarian. Since there are many tasks that must get done in order to make materials available to users, you must have excellent time-management skills. Technicians who supervise the work of others must be able to manage effectively, explain procedures, set deadlines, and follow through with subordinates. You should also feel comfortable reporting to supervisors and working alongside other technicians in a team atmosphere.

EXPLORING

Personal experience as a library patron is the first opportunity for you to see if a library career would be of interest. You can get a good idea of the general atmosphere of a library by browsing for books, searching in electronic encyclopedias for a school research project, or using a library's Internet connection to access all kinds of information. Using libraries yourself will also give you an idea of the types of services that a library provides for its patrons.

If you are interested in a career as a library technician, talk with your school and community librarians and library technicians. A visit to a large or specialized library would also be helpful in providing a view of the different kinds of libraries that exist.

There may also be opportunities to work as a library volunteer at a public library or in the school library media center. Some grammar schools or high schools have library clubs as a part of their extracurricular activities. If your school doesn't have a library club, contact your school librarian and get some friends together to start your own group. Part-time or summer work as a shelving clerk or typist may also be available in some libraries.

EMPLOYERS

There are approximately 109,000 library technicians employed in the United States. Most library technicians work in grammar school, high school, college, university, and public libraries. The rest work for government libraries, in special libraries for privately held institutions, or in corporate repositories. Many types of organizations employ library technicians. For example, library technicians are key personnel at archives, zoos, museums, hospitals, fraternal organizations, historical societies, medical centers, law firms, professional societies, advertising agencies, and virtual libraries. In general, wherever there is a library, library technicians are needed.

STARTING OUT

Since specific training requirements vary from library to library, if you are interested in a career as a library technician, you should be familiar with the requirements of the libraries in which you hope to work. In some small libraries, for instance, a high school diploma may be sufficient, and a technician might not need a college degree. However, since most libraries require their library technicians to be graduates of at least a two-year associate's degree program, you should have earned or be close to earning this degree before applying.

In most cases, graduates of training programs for library technicians may seek employment through the placement offices of their community colleges. Job applicants may also approach libraries directly, usually by contacting the personnel officer of the library or the human resources administrator of the organization. Civil service examination notices, for those interested in government service, are usually posted in community colleges as well as in government buildings and on government websites.

Many state library agencies maintain job hotlines listing openings for prospective library technicians. State departments of education also may keep lists of openings available for library technicians. If you are interested in working in a school library media center, you should remember that most openings occur at the end of the school year and are filled for the following year.

ADVANCEMENT

The trend toward requiring more formal training for library technicians suggests that advancement opportunities will be limited for those lacking such training. In smaller libraries and less-populated areas, the shortage of trained personnel may lessen this limitation. Nonetheless, those with adequate or above-average training will perform the more interesting tasks.

Generally, library technicians advance by taking on greater levels of responsibility. A new technician, for instance, may check materials in and out at the library's circulation desk and then move on to inputting, storing, and verifying information. Experienced technicians in supervisory roles might be responsible for budgets and personnel or the operation of an entire department. Library technicians will find that experience, along with continuing education courses, will enhance their chances for advancement.

Library technicians might also advance by pursuing a master's degree in library and information science and becoming a librarian. With experience, additional courses, or an advanced degree, technicians can also advance to higher paying positions outside of the library setting.

EARNINGS

Salaries for library technicians vary depending on such factors as the type of library, geographic location, and specific job responsibilities. According to the U.S. Department of Labor, the median annual salary for all library technicians in 2001 was $23,790. The lowest paid 10 percent made less than $14,190, while the highest paid 10 percent earned more than $37,420. The U.S. Department of Labor also reported that library technicians working for the federal government averaged an annual salary of about $33,224 in 2001.

Benefits vary according to employer, but most full-time library technicians receive the same benefits as other employees, which may include the following: health insurance, dental insurance, paid vacations, paid holidays, compensated sick time, and retirement savings plans. Library technicians in grammar schools and high schools generally work fewer hours during summers and holidays when students are not in class, although these "down" times are often used to finish up backlogged projects. Technicians who work in corporate libraries may receive special perks as part of their benefits plan, such as stock in the company or discounts on products the company produces or markets. Many colleges and universities offer their employees discounted or free classes to help them earn a higher degree. Most employers offer training sessions to their technicians to keep them informed of new developments in library services and technology.

WORK ENVIRONMENT

Libraries are usually clean, well-lit, pleasant work atmospheres. Hours are regular in company libraries and in school library media centers, but academic, public, and some specialized libraries are open longer hours and may require evening and weekend work, usually on a rotating basis.

Some tasks performed by library technicians, like calculating circulation statistics, can be repetitive. Technicians working in technical services may develop headaches and eyestrain from working long hours in front of a computer screen. Heavy public contact in user services may test a technician's tact and patience. However, a library's atmosphere is generally relaxed and interesting. The size and type of library will often determine the duties of library technicians. A technician working in a small branch library might handle a wide range of responsibilities. Sometimes a technician working in a school, rural, or special library might be the senior staff member, with full responsibility for all technical, user, and administrative services and staff supervision. A technician working in a large university or public library might focus on only one task all of the time.

Libraries are presently responding to decreased government funding by cutting budgets and reducing staff, often leaving an overwhelming workload for the remaining staff members. Because library technicians earn less money than librarians do, libraries often replace librarians with technicians. This situation can lead to resentment in the working relationship among colleagues. In addition, there is also an ongoing struggle to define the different responsibilities of the librarian and technician. Despite the difference in the educational requirements for the two jobs—librarians require a master's degree and technicians an associate's degree—some of the responsibilities do overlap. Library technicians may find it frustrating that, in some cases, they are performing the same tasks as librarians and yet do not command the same salary.

OUTLOOK

The U.S. Department of Labor predicts employment for library technicians to grow about as fast as the average over the next several years. Job openings will result from technicians leaving the field for other employment or retirement, as well as from libraries looking to stretch their budgets. Since a library technician earns less than a librarian, a library may find it more economical to hire the technician. The continued growth of special libraries in medical, business, and law organizations will lead to growing opportunities for technicians who develop specialized skills. A technician who has excellent computer skills and is able to learn quickly will be highly employable, as will a technician who shows the drive to gain advanced degrees and accept more responsibility.

FOR MORE INFORMATION

For information on library careers, a list of accredited schools, scholarships and grants, and college student membership, contact:
American Library Association
50 East Huron Street
Chicago, IL 60611
Tel: 800-545-2433
Email: ala@ala.org
http://www.ala.org

For information on education and awards programs, contact:
Association for Educational Communications and Technology
1800 North Stonelake Drive, Suite 2
Bloomington, IN 47408
Tel: 877-677-2328
Email: aect@aect.org
http://www.aect.org

For information on continuing education programs and publications, contact:
Library & Information Technology Association
c/o American Library Association
50 East Huron Street
Chicago, IL 60611-2795
Tel: 800-545-2433, ext. 4270
Email: lita@ala.org
http://www.lita.org

For information on the wide variety of careers in special libraries, contact:
Special Libraries Association
1700 18th Street, NW
Washington, DC 20009-2514
Tel: 202-234-4700
Email: sla@sla.org
http://www.sla.org

For information on library technician careers in Canada, contact:
Alberta Association of Library Technicians
PO Box 700
Edmonton, AB T5J 2L4 Canada
http://www.aalt.org

To request information on education programs in Canada and scholarships, contact:
Canadian Library Association
328 Frank Street
Ottawa, ON K2P 0X8 Canada
Tel: 613-232-9625
Email: info@cla.ca
http://www.cla.ca

Medical Secretaries

OVERVIEW

Medical secretaries are responsible for the administrative and clerical work in medical offices, hospitals, or private physicians' offices. They answer phone calls, order supplies, handle correspondence, bill patients, complete insurance forms, and transcribe dictation. Medical secretaries also handle bookkeeping, greet patients, schedule appointments, arrange hospital admissions, and schedule surgeries. There are approximately 314,000 medical secretaries employed throughout the United States.

HISTORY

No one knows exactly when secretarial positions originated. Members of the nobility had secretaries (always men) who had command of several languages, including Latin, and were required to have what we would consider today to be a broad, generalized education.

During the industrial expansion at the turn of the century, businesses faced a paperwork crisis. Secretaries helped to solve this problem, using new technologies such as adding machines, telephones, and typewriters. Many people aspired to hold positions as secretaries. In the 1930s, the number of male secretaries dwindled, and women began to dominate the office workforce.

Today, secretaries, also known as *administrative assistants, office coordinators, executive assistants*, and *office managers*, are more technologically driven, using computers, the Internet, and other equipment to perform vital information-management functions.

QUICK FACTS

School Subjects
English
Health
Speech

Personal Skills
Communication/ideas
Following instructions

Work Environment
Primarily indoors
Primarily one location

Minimum Education Level
High school diploma

Salary Range
$17,650 to $31,906 to $40,000+

Certification or Licensing
Voluntary

Outlook
About as fast as the average

DOT
201

GOE
07.01.03

NOC
1243

O*NET-SOC
43-6013.00

THE JOB

Medical secretaries play important roles in the health care profession. They transcribe dictation, prepare correspondence, and assist physicians or medical scientists with reports, speeches, articles, and conference proceedings. Medical secretaries also record simple medical histories, arrange for patients to be hospitalized, and order supplies. Most need to be familiar with insurance rules, billing practices, and hospital or laboratory procedures.

Doctors rely on medical secretaries to keep administrative operations under control. Secretaries are the information clearinghouses for the office. They schedule appointments, handle phone calls, organize and maintain paper and electronic files, and produce correspondence for the office. Medical secretaries must have basic technical skills to operate office equipment such as facsimile machines, photocopiers, and switchboard systems. Increasingly, they use computers to run spreadsheet, word-processing, database-management, or desktop publishing programs.

REQUIREMENTS

High School

Most employers require medical secretaries to have a high school diploma and be able to type between 60 and 90 words per minute. In order to handle more specialized duties, you must be familiar with medical terms and procedures and be able to use medical software programs. In addition, you need to have basic math skills and strong written and verbal communication skills to write up correspondence and handle patient inquiries. English, speech, and health classes will help you prepare for this career.

Postsecondary Training

One and two-year programs are offered by many vocational, community, and business schools covering the skills needed for secretarial work. For more specialized training, some schools offer medical secretarial programs, covering the basics such as typing, filing, and accounting, as well as more specialized courses on medical stenography, first aid, medical terminology, and medical office procedures.

Certification or Licensing

Certification is not required for a job as a medical secretary, but obtaining it may bring increased opportunities, earnings, and responsibility. The International Association of Administrative Professionals offers the Certified Professional Secretary (CPS) designation. To achieve CPS certification, you must meet certain experience requirements and pass a rigorous exam covering a number of general secretarial topics.

Other Requirements
To succeed as a medical secretary, you must be trustworthy and use discretion when dealing with confidential medical records. You must also have a pleasant and confident personality for handling the public and a desire to help others in a dependable and conscientious manner.

EXPLORING

The best way to learn about this career is to speak with an experienced medical secretary about his or her work. Ask your school guidance counselor to set up an information interview with a medical secretary, or arrange a tour of a medical facility so you can see secretaries in action.

EMPLOYERS

Approximately 314,000 medical secretaries are employed in the United States. Medical secretaries work in private physicians' offices, hospitals, outpatient clinics, emergency care facilities, research laboratories, and large health organizations, such as the Mayo Medical Clinic. The Mayo Clinic branches, located in Florida, Minnesota, and Arizona, employ more than 1,000 medical secretaries who work for nearly 1,200 physicians and scientists. The majority work with one or two physicians practicing in a clinical outpatient care setting. The rest provide support to physicians and scientists in clinical and research laboratories, hospitals, or Mayo Clinic's medical school.

STARTING OUT

To find work in this field, you should apply directly to hospitals, clinics, and physicians' offices. Potential positions might be listed with school or college placement centers or in newspaper want ads. Networking with medical secretaries is another inside track to job leads, because employers tend to trust employee recommendations.

ADVANCEMENT

Promotions for secretaries who work in doctors' offices are usually limited to increases in salary and responsibilities. Medical secretaries employed by clinics or hospitals can advance to executive positions, such as senior secretary, clerical supervisor, or office manager; or into more administrative jobs, such as medical records clerk, administrative assistant, or unit manager.

EARNINGS

According to 2002 Wageweb data, the average salary for medical secretaries was approximately $31,906 per year. Beginning workers earned an average of $24,088; more experienced secretaries earned an average of $40,001.

The U.S. Department of Labor reports that medical secretaries earned a median annual salary of $24,670 in 2001. Salaries ranged from less than $17,650 to more than $36,520.

Most employers offer vacation, sick leave, and medical benefits. Many also include life, dental, and vision care insurance, retirement benefits, and profit sharing.

WORK ENVIRONMENT

Medical secretaries usually work 40 hours a week, Monday through Friday, during regular business hours. However, some work extended hours one or two days a week, depending on the physician's office hours. They do their work in well-lit, pleasant surroundings, but could encounter stressful emergency situations.

OUTLOOK

While the demand for secretaries in the general sector is expected to show little change or grow more slowly than the average for all occupations, the U.S. Department of Labor projects a higher demand for medical secretaries, expecting the occupation to grow as fast as the average over the next several years.

Health services are demanding more from their support personnel and are increasing salary levels accordingly. Technological advances are making secretaries more productive and able to handle the duties once done by managers or other staff. The distribution of work has shifted; secretaries receive fewer requests for typing and filing jobs. Instead, they do more technical work requiring computer skills beyond keyboarding. The job outlook looks brightest for those who are up to date on the latest programs and technological advances.

FOR MORE INFORMATION

For information on training to become a medical secretary, contact:
Arlington Career Institute
901 Avenue K
Grand Prairie, TX 75050
Tel: 800-394-5445
Email: ACRI1@swbell.net
http://www.themetro.com/aci

For information on professional certification, contact:
International Association of Administrative Professionals
PO Box 20404
10502 NW Ambassador Drive
Kansas City, MO 64195-0404
Tel: 816-891-6600
Email: service@iaap-hq.org
http://www.iaap-hq.org

The Mayo Clinic is a major employer of medical secretaries. Visit their website for more information.
Mayo Clinic
http://www.mayo.edu

Medical Transcriptionists

QUICK FACTS

School Subjects
Biology
English
Health

Personal Skills
Communication/ideas
Technical/scientific

Work Environment
Primarily indoors
Primarily one location

Minimum Education Level
Some postsecondary training

Salary Range
$18,760 to $31,400 to
$36,225+

Certification or Licensing
Recommended

Outlook
Faster than the average

DOT
N/A

GOE
N/A

NOC
1244

O*NET-SOC
31-9094.00

OVERVIEW

Doctors and other health care professionals often make tape recordings documenting what happened during their patients' appointments or surgical procedures. *Medical transcriptionists* listen to these tapes and transcribe, or type, reports of what the doctor said. The reports are then included in patients' charts. Medical transcriptionists work in a variety of health care settings, including hospitals, clinics, and doctors' offices, as well as for transcription companies or out of their own homes. There are about 94,100 medical transcriptionists working in the United States. Medical transcriptionists are also called *medical transcribers, medical stenographers,* or *medical language specialists.*

HISTORY

Health care documentation dates back to the beginnings of medical treatment. Doctors used to keep their own handwritten records of a patient's medical history and treatment. After 1900, medical stenographers took on this role. Stenographers worked alongside doctors, writing down doctors' reports in shorthand. This changed with the invention of the dictating machine, which led to the development of the career of medical transcription.

The first commercial dictating machine, using a wax cylinder record, was produced in 1887. It was based on Thomas A. Edison's (1847–1931) phonograph invented in 1877. Technology has come a long way since then. Recent advances in the field include Internet transcription capabilities and voice- (or speech-) recognition software. The latter electronically transcribes recorded spoken word, which means that a medical transcriptionist does not have to type out all the dictation. Given the complexity of medical terminology, however, voice recognition programs are likely to make mistakes, so there is still plenty of work for the medical transcriptionist, who must carefully proofread the report to catch and correct any errors.

THE JOB

Medical transcriptionists transcribe (type into printed format) a dictated (oral) report recorded by a doctor or another health care professional. They work for primary care physicians as well as health care professionals in various medical specialties, including cardiology, immunology, oncology, podiatry, radiology, and urology. The medical transcriptionist usually types up the report while listening to the recording through a transcriber machine's headset, using a foot pedal to stop or rewind the recording as necessary. Some doctors dictate over the telephone, and others use the Internet.

The report consists of information gathered during a patient's office appointment or hospital visit and covers the patient's medical history and treatment. Doctors dictate information about patient consultations, physical examinations, results from laboratory work or X rays, medical tests, psychiatric evaluations, patient diagnosis and prognosis, surgical procedures, a patient's hospital stay and discharge, autopsies, and so on. Often doctors will use abbreviations while dictating. The medical transcriptionist must type out the full names of those abbreviations.

Because the report becomes a permanent part of a patient's medical record and is referred to by the same doctor or other members of the patient's health care team during future office visits or when determining future medical treatment, it must be accurate. This includes dates and the spelling of medications, procedures, diseases, medical instruments and supplies, and laboratory values.

After typing up a report, medical transcriptionists review it and make corrections to grammar, punctuation, and spelling. They read it to be sure it is clear, consistent, and complete and does not contain any errors. Medical transcriptionists are expected to edit for clarity and make grammar corrections; therefore, the final report does not need to be identical to the original dictation in those respects.

Being a medical transcriptionist is not all about typing and proofreading. Medical transcriptionists are very familiar with medical terminology. When recording their reports, doctors use medical terms that are relevant to a patient's condition and treatment. Such terms might be names of diseases or medications. Medical transcriptionists understand what these medical terms mean and how they are spelled. They understand enough about various diseases and their symptoms, treatments, and prognoses as to be able to figure out what a doctor is saying if the recording is a little garbled. They have a good understanding of medicine and know about human anatomy and physiology. If what the doctor says on the tape is unclear, a medical transcriptionist often has to determine the appropriate word or words based on the context. However, medical transcriptionists never guess when it comes to medications, conditions, medical history, and treatments. A patient could receive improper and even damaging treatment if a diagnosis is made based on a report containing errors. Medical transcriptionists contact the doctor if they are uncertain or they leave a blank in the report, depending on the employer's or client's expectations and guidelines. After the medical transcriptionist reviews the report, it is given to the doctor, who also reviews it and then signs it if it is acceptable—or returns it to the transcriptionist for correction, if necessary. Once it has been signed, the report is placed in the patient's permanent medical file.

Many medical transcriptionists use voice recognition software to create documents electronically from oral dictation, eliminating much of their typing work. Medical transcriptionists still have to review the transcription for accuracy and format.

While some transcriptionists only do transcribing, other transcriptionists, often those who work in doctors' offices or clinics, may have additional responsibilities. They may deal with patients, answer the phone, handle the mail, and perform other clerical tasks. And transcriptionists may be asked to file or deliver the reports to other doctors, lawyers, or other people who request them.

A growing number of medical transcriptionists work out of their homes, either telecommuting as employees or subcontractors or as self-employed workers. As technology becomes more sophisticated, this trend is likely to continue. Medical transcriptionists who work out of their homes have some degree of mobility and can live where they choose, taking their jobs with them. These workers must keep up to date with their medical resources and equipment. Because terminology continues to change, medical transcriptionists regularly buy revised editions of some of the standard medical resources.

REQUIREMENTS

High School

English and grammar classes are important in preparing you to become a medical transcriptionist. Focus on becoming a better speller.

If you understand the meanings of word prefixes and suffixes (many of which come from Greek and Latin), it will be easier for you to learn medical terminology, since many terms are formed by adding a prefix and/or a suffix to a word or root. If your high school offers Greek or Latin classes, take one; otherwise, try to take Greek or Latin when you continue your studies after high school.

Biology and health classes will give you a solid introduction to the human body and how it functions, preparing you to take more advanced classes in anatomy and physiology after you graduate. Be sure to learn how to type by taking a class or teaching yourself. Practice typing regularly to build up your speed and accuracy. Word-processing and computer classes are also useful.

Postsecondary Training

Some junior, community, and business colleges and vocational schools have medical transcription programs. You can also learn the business of medical transcription by taking a correspondence course. To be accepted into a medical transcription program, you might need to have a minimum typing speed. The American Association for Medical Transcription (AAMT) recommends that medical transcriptionists complete a two-year program offering an associate's degree, but this is not necessary for you to find a job.

You should take courses in English grammar as well as medical terminology, anatomy, physiology, and pharmacology. Some of the more specific classes you might take include medicolegal concepts and ethics, human disease and pathophysiology, health care records management, and medical grammar and editing. Certain programs offer on-the-job training, which will help when you are looking for full-time employment.

The AAMT has a mentoring program for students who are studying medical transcription. Students can make important contacts in the field and learn much from experienced professionals.

Certification or Licensing

The Medical Transcription Certification Commission (MTCC) of the AAMT administers a two-part certification examination. Those who pass the exam become Certified Medical Transcriptionists (CMT's). Certification is good for three years, at which point recertification is necessary to keep the CMT. designation. At least 30 hours of continuing education credits are required every three years. (There are also certain other requirements, which are detailed at the AAMT website, http://www.aamt.org.)

While medical transcriptionists do not need to be certified to find a job, it is highly recommended as a sign of achievement and professionalism. CMT's will probably more readily find employment and earn higher salaries.

Other Requirements

A love of language and grammar is an important quality, and accuracy and attention to detail are absolute musts for a medical transcriptionist. It is essential that you correctly type up information as spoken by the doctor on the tape recording. You must be able to sift through background sounds on the tape and accurately record what the doctor says. Doctors dictate at the same time they are with a patient or later from their office or maybe even as they go about their daily routine, perhaps while eating, driving in traffic, or walking along a busy street. In each of these cases, the recording will likely include background noises or conversations that at times drown out or make unclear what the doctor is saying.

Many doctors grew up outside of the United States and do not speak English as their first language, so they may not have a thorough understanding of English or they may speak with an accent. You must have a good ear to be able to decipher what these doctors are saying.

In addition to having accurate typing skills, you will also need to type quickly if you want to make higher wages and get more clients. A solid understanding of word-processing software will help you to be more productive. An example of this is the use of macros, or keystroke combinations that are used for repetitive actions, such as typing the same long, hard-to-spell word or phrase time and again. If you suffer from repetitive strain injuries, then this would not be a suitable profession.

Flexibility is also important because you must be able to adapt to the different skills and needs of various health care professionals.

Medical transcriptionists should be able to concentrate and be prepared to sit in one place for long periods at a time, either typing or reading. For this reason, it is important that you take regular breaks. An ability to work independently will help you whether you are self-employed or have an office position, since you do most of your work sitting at a computer.

Medical transcriptionists are required to keep patient records confidential, just as doctors are, so integrity and discretion are important.

EXPLORING

There is plenty of accessible reading material aimed at medical transcriptionists. This is a good way to learn more about the field and decide if it sounds interesting to you. Several of the websites listed at the end of this article feature self-tests and articles about medical transcription. Marylou Bunting, a home-based certified medical transcriptionist, recommends that you get a medical dictionary and *Physicians' Desk Reference (PDR)* to familiarize yourself with terminology. See if your local library has the *Journal of the American Association for Medical Transcription* and browse through some issues. The Internet is a great resource for would-be medical transcriptionists. Find a bulletin board or mailing list and talk to professionals in the field, perhaps conducting an informational interview.

Bunting also suggests that you "put yourself in a medical setting as soon and as often as you can." Ask if your doctor can use your help in any way or apply for a volunteer position at a local hospital. Ask to be assigned to the hospital's medical records department, which won't give you the opportunity to transcribe, but will give you some experience dealing with medical records.

EMPLOYERS

According to the *Occupational Outlook Handbook,* there are about 94,100 medical transcriptionists working in the United States. About two of five work in hospitals and two of five work in doctors' offices and clinics. Others work for laboratories, medical centers, colleges and universities, medical libraries, insurance companies, transcription companies, temp agencies, and even veterinary facilities. Medical transcriptionists can also find government jobs, with public health or veterans hospitals.

STARTING OUT

It can be difficult to get started in this field, especially if you do not have any work experience. Some medical transcriptionists start out working as administrative assistants or receptionists in doctors' offices. They become acquainted with medical terminology and office procedures, and they make important contacts in the medical profession. According to AAMT, a smaller doctor's office may be more apt to hire an inexperienced medical transcriptionist than a hospital or transcription service would be.

Marylou Bunting recommends that you try to get an apprenticeship position since on-the-job experience seems to be a prerequisite for most jobs. Or perhaps you can find an internship position with a transcription company. Once you have some experience, you can look for another position through classified ads, job search agencies, or Internet resources. You can also find job leads through word-of-mouth and professional contacts. The AAMT website features job postings. In fact, AAMT is an invaluable resource for the medical transcriptionist. Local chapters hold periodic meetings, which is a good way to network with other professionals in the field.

ADVANCEMENT

There are few actual advancement opportunities for medical transcriptionists. Those who become faster and more accurate will have an easier time securing better-paying positions or lining up new clients. Skilled and experienced medical transcriptionists can become supervisors of transcription departments or managers of transcription companies, or they might even form their own transcription companies. Some also become teachers, consultants, or authors or editors of books on the subject of medical transcription.

EARNINGS

Medical transcriptionists are paid in a variety of ways, depending on the employer or client. Payment might be made based on the number of hours worked or the number of lines transcribed. Monetary incentives might be offered to hourly transcriptionists achieving a high rate of production.

According to a 2002 member survey conducted by the American Association for Medical Transcription, medical transcriptionists earned an average annual salary of $31,400. The U.S. Department of Labor reports that in 2001 the lowest 10 percent of all medical transcriptionists made less than $9.02 per hour (or an annual salary of about $18,760), and the highest 10 percent made more than $17.51 per hour (about $36,430 annually). Medical transcriptionists who worked for mailing, reproduction, and stenographic services earned a median hourly wage of $11.47 in 2000. Those employed in hospitals earned $12.14 an hour and those who worked in offices and clinics of medical doctors earned $12.25 an hour in 2000.

Medical transcriptionists who are certified earn higher average salaries than transcriptionists who have not earned certification. The magazine *Advance for Health Information Professionals* reports that certified medical transcriptionists earned an average of $36,225 in 2002.

Medical transcriptionists working in a hospital or company setting can expect to have the usual benefits, including paid vacation, sick days, and health insurance. Tuition reimbursement and 401-K plans may also be offered. Home-based medical transcriptionists who are employed by a company may be entitled to the same benefits that in-house staff members get. It is important to check with each individual company to be sure. Self-employed medical transcriptionists have to make arrangements for their own health and retirement plans and other benefits.

WORK ENVIRONMENT

Most medical transcriptionists work in an office setting, either at their employer's place of business or in their own homes. They generally sit at desks in front of computers and have transcribers or dictation machines and medical reference books at hand. Home-based workers and sometimes even office workers must invest a substantial amount of money in reference books and equipment on an ongoing basis, to keep up with changes in medical terminology and technology.

Transcriptionists who are not self-employed usually put in a 40-hour week. Some medical transcriptionists working in hospitals are assigned to the second or third shift. Independent contractors, on the other hand, clock their hours when they have work to do. Sometimes this will be part-time or on the weekends or at night. If they are busy enough, some work more hours than in the normal workweek.

Because medical transcriptionists spend such a long time typing at a computer, the risk of repetitive stress injuries is present. Other physical problems may also occur, including eyestrain from staring at a computer screen and back or neck pain from sitting in one position for long periods at a time.

OUTLOOK

As Internet security issues are resolved, its use for receiving dictation and returning transcriptions will likely become more popular. The Internet offers a quick way to communicate and transfer documents, which is useful for medical transcriptionists who work far away from their employers or clients. As voice-recognition technology improves and better recognizes complex medical terminology, it, too, will be used more and medical transcriptionists will do less typing.

Even with these technological advances, there will continue to be a need for medical transcriptionists. They will still have to review electronically created documents. And given that people are living longer, they will require more medical tests and procedures, which will all need to be documented and transcribed. The U.S. Department of Labor reports that employment of medical transcriptionists is expected to grow faster than the average over the next several years.

FOR MORE INFORMATION

AAMT, a professional organization for medical transcriptionists, provides many online resources, including suggestions on how to prepare for a career in medical transcription, a career overview, tips for students, and tips for those interested in becoming self-employed medical transcriptionists.

American Association for
   Medical Transcription (AAMT)
100 Sycamore Avenue
Modesto, CA 95354-0550
Tel: 800-982-2182
Email: aamt@aamt.org
http://www.aamt.org

This publication contains an assortment of articles of interest to health information management professionals, including medical transcriptionists.

Advance for Health Information Professionals
http://www.advanceforhim.com

This website features articles and resources for medical transcriptionists and those wanting to learn more about the field.

Keeping Abreast of Medical Transcription
http://www.wwma.com/kamt

For an overview of the job, several language resources and tests, and sample reports, visit:

Medword—Medical Transcription
http://www.medword.com

This networking resource for professionals includes discussion forums and interviews.

MT Daily
http://www.mtdaily.com

See this website for an extensive glossary, a huge list of "stumper terms" for medical transcriptionists, links to other medical-related dictionaries and resources, sample operative reports, book suggestions, chat forums, and classified ads.

MT Desk
http://www.mtdesk.com

This site features preparatory materials, including quizzes, proofreading tests, and crossword puzzles; articles about getting started; tips on transcribing, punctuation, and grammar; and listings of recommended resources.

MT Monthly and Review of Systems School of Medical
    Transcription
http://www.mtmonthly.com

INTERVIEW

Kim Buchanan is a certified medical transcriptionist. Buchanan spoke with the editors of Careers in Focus: Clerks & Administrative Workers *about her career and the field of medical transcription in general.*

Q. Please briefly describe your job duties.

A. I am currently employed as a mentor for a national transcription service. I work with newly hired employees to help transition them to our software and accounts. My primary duties include educating employees regarding my company's style preferences, troubleshooting technical support issues, providing feedback on production and quality, and a lot of general hand-holding. I also work closely with the proofreading staff to establish standards and provide consistent feedback to the employees.

Q. Can you describe your work atmosphere? Do you travel for your job?

A. I work indoors, out of a home office. I do minimal travel for my job—perhaps once a year for training.

Q. How did you train for this job? What was your college major?

A. I do have a college degree (in social work, with a minor in business), but for my transcription career I attended a nine-month certificate program at a local technical college. I have also taken college-level anatomy and physiology classes and participated in hundreds of hours of continuing education in order to obtain and maintain my certified medical transcriptionist credential.

Q. Did you participate in any internships while you were in college?

A. Yes—at a family counseling center—working with troubled young people as well as with an anger-management program.

Q. How/where did you get your first job in this field? What did you do?

A. I was hired right out of my transcription program by a small local transcription service. I began transcribing immediately.

Q. How can an aspiring medical transcriptionist find his or her first job in the field?

A. There are always ads in the papers; however, in my experience, the majority of available transcription work is distributed via word-of-mouth and through advertising in publications (such as the Journal for *American Medical Transcriptionists, Advance,* and *For the Record*) related to our profession.

Q. What are the most important personal and professional qualities for people in your career?

A. Excellent English grammar, strong understanding of medical terminology, an "ear" for dictation, persistence, flexibility, and attention to detail.

Q. What are some of the pros and cons of your job?

A. Pros: The medical field, as well as the technology involved in our profession, is ever-changing. You never stop learning. There are a variety of work environments. This is definitely not a one-size-fits-all profession. There seems to be an unending amount of work so we all have job security. Personally, the biggest pro of my job is that I am able to work from home for a company that supports me personally and professionally. I get to work with people that I respect, and I feel like I'm really helping to make a difference in people's lives as they enter this profession.

Cons: The biggest con of my profession is the constant battle for better pay. Hand-in-hand with that, we often fight for respect from our fellow healthcare professionals. We struggle with the perception that we are "typists."

Q. What advice would you give a young person entering this field?

A. Get involved in your professional association (the American Association for Medical Transcription). Not only will you develop strong networking relationships with other professionals in this field, but you will receive the continuing education that is so vital.

Q. What is the future employment outlook for medical transcription?

A. Extremely favorable. The Bureau of Labor Statistics states that this profession will continue to grow over the next 10 years. Personally, I believe that there will always be more work than there are qualified transcriptionists to do the job.

Office Clerks

OVERVIEW

Office clerks perform a variety of clerical tasks that help an office run smoothly, including file maintenance, mail sorting, and record-keeping. In large companies, office clerks might have specialized tasks such as inputting data into a computer, but in most cases, clerks are flexible and have many duties including typing, answering telephones, taking messages, making photocopies, and preparing mailings. Office clerks usually work under close supervision, often with experienced clerks directing their activities. There are approximately 2.7 million office clerks employed in the United States.

HISTORY

Before the 18th century, many businesspeople did their own office work, such as shipping products, accepting payments, and recording inventory. The Industrial Revolution changed the nature of business by popularizing the specialization of labor, which allowed companies to increase their output dramatically. At this time, office clerks were brought in to handle the growing amount of clerical duties.

Office workers have become more important as computers, word processors, and other technological advances have increased both the volume of business information available and the speed with which administrative decisions can be made. The number of office workers in the United States has grown as more trained personnel are needed to handle the volume of business communication and information. Businesses and government agencies depend on skilled office workers to file and sort documents, operate office equipment, and cooperate with others to ensure the flow of information.

Keeping files organized and up to date is a large part of an office clerk's job. *(Ken Hammond/USDA)*

THE JOB

Office clerks usually perform a variety of tasks as part of their overall job responsibility. They may type or file bills, statements, and business correspondence. They may stuff envelopes, answer telephones, and sort mail. Office clerks also enter data into computers, run errands, and operate office equipment such as photocopiers, fax machines, and switchboards. In the course of an average day, an office clerk usually performs a combination of these and other clerical tasks, spending an hour or so on one task and then moving on to another as directed by an office manager or other supervisor.

An office clerk may work with other office personnel, such as a bookkeeper or accountant, to maintain a company's financial records. The clerk may type and mail invoices and sort payments as they come in, keep payroll records, or take inventories. With more experience, the clerk may be asked to update customer files to reflect receipt of payments and verify records for accuracy.

Office clerks often deliver messages from one office worker to another, an especially important responsibility in larger companies.

Clerks may relay questions and answers from one department head to another. Similarly, clerks may relay messages from people outside the company or employees who are outside of the office to those working in house. Office clerks may also work with other personnel on individual projects, such as preparing a yearly budget or making sure a mass mailing gets out on time.

Administrative clerks assist in the efficient operation of an office by compiling business records; providing information to sales personnel and customers; and preparing and sending out bills, policies, invoices, and other business correspondence. Administrative clerks may also keep financial records and prepare the payroll. *File clerks* review and classify letters, documents, articles, and other information and then file this material so it can be quickly retrieved at a later time. They contribute to the smooth distribution of information at a company.

Some clerks have titles that describe where they work and the jobs they do. For example, *congressional-district aides* work for the elected officials of their U.S. congressional district. *Police clerks* handle routine office procedures in police stations, and *concrete products dispatchers* work with construction firms on building projects.

REQUIREMENTS

High School
To prepare for a career as an office clerk, you should take courses in English, mathematics, and as many business-related subjects, such as keyboarding and bookkeeping, as possible. Community colleges and vocational schools often offer business education courses that provide training for general office workers.

Postsecondary Training
A high school diploma is usually sufficient for beginning office clerks, although business courses covering office machine operation and bookkeeping are also helpful. To succeed in this field, you should have computer skills, the ability to concentrate for long periods of time on repetitive tasks, good English and communication skills, and mathematical abilities. Legible handwriting is also a necessity.

Other Requirements
To find work as an office clerk, you should have an even temperament, strong communication skills, and the ability to work well with others. You should find systematic and detailed work appealing. Other personal qualifications include dependability, trustworthiness, and a neat personal appearance.

EXPLORING

You can gain experience by taking on clerical or bookkeeping responsibilities with a school club or other organization. In addition, some school work-study programs may provide opportunities for part-time on-the-job training with local businesses. You may also be able to get a part-time or summer job in a business office by contacting businesses directly or enlisting the aid of a guidance counselor. Training in the operation of business machinery (computers, word processors, and so on) may be available through evening courses offered by business schools and community colleges.

EMPLOYERS

Approximately 2.7 million office clerks are employed throughout the United States. Major employers include utility companies, insurance agencies, and finance, real estate, and other large firms. Smaller companies also hire office workers and sometimes offer a greater opportunity to gain experience in a variety of clerical tasks.

STARTING OUT

When you are interested in securing an entry-level position, you should contact businesses or government agencies directly. Newspaper ads and temporary-work agencies are also good sources for finding jobs in this area. Most companies provide on-the-job training, during which company policies and procedures are explained.

ADVANCEMENT

Office clerks usually begin their employment performing more routine tasks such as delivering messages and sorting and filing mail. With experience, they may advance to more complicated assignments and assume a greater responsibility for the entire project to be completed. Those who demonstrate the desire and ability may move to other clerical positions, such as secretary or receptionist. Clerks with good leadership skills may become group managers or supervisors. To be promoted to a professional occupation such as accountant, a college degree or other specialized training is usually necessary.

The high turnover rate that exists among office clerks increases promotional opportunities. The number and kind of opportunities, however, usually depend on the place of employment and the ability, education, and experience of the employee.

EARNINGS

Salaries for office clerks vary depending on the size and geographic location of the company and the skills of the worker. According to the U.S. Department of Labor, the median salary for full-time office clerks was $21,780 in 2001. The lowest paid 10 percent earned less than $13,980, while the highest paid group earned more than $34,090.

According to a 2002 salary survey by OfficeTeam, office assistants earned between $19,250 and $22,500, while senior office assistants earned up to $25,250.

Full-time workers generally also receive paid vacations, health insurance, sick leave, and other benefits.

WORK ENVIRONMENT

As is the case with most office workers, office clerks work an average 37- to 40-hour week. They usually work in comfortable surroundings and are provided with modern equipment. Although clerks have a variety of tasks and responsibilities, the job itself can be fairly routine and repetitive. Clerks often interact with accountants and other office personnel and may work under close supervision.

OUTLOOK

Nearly 3 million people hold jobs as office clerks. Although employment of clerks is expected to grow only about as fast as the average over the next several years, there will still be many jobs available due to the vastness of this field and a high turnover rate. With the increased use of data processing equipment and other types of automated office machinery, more and more employers are hiring people proficient in a variety of office tasks. According to OfficeTeam, the following industries show the strongest demand for qualified administrative staff: technology, financial services, construction, and manufacturing.

Because they are so versatile, office workers can find employment in virtually any kind of industry, so their overall employment does not depend on the fortunes of any single sector of the economy. In addition to private companies, the federal government should continue to be a good source of jobs. Employment opportunities should be especially good for those trained in various computer skills as well as other office machinery. Temporary and part-time work opportunities should also increase, especially during busy business periods.

FOR MORE INFORMATION

For information on seminars, conferences, and news on the industry, contact:

National Association of Executive Secretaries and Administrative Assistants
900 South Washington Street, Suite G-13
Falls Church, VA 22046
Tel: 703-237-8616
http://www.naesaa.com

For free office career and salary information, visit the following website:

OfficeTeam
http://www.officeteam.com

Railroad Clerks

OVERVIEW

Railroad clerks perform the clerical duties involved in transacting business and keeping records for railroad companies. Their jobs may involve many different kinds of clerical work or only one or two specialized duties, depending on the size and type of their railroad company or location.

HISTORY

The modern era of railroading began in the early 1800s, when two Englishmen, Richard Trevithick and George Stephenson, perfected their versions of the steam locomotive. In the early days, railroads were largely short lines, and a few clerks could keep track of the trains' cargo and destinations. But as railroads expanded, both geographically and in the types of freight they could carry, clerks became essential to keep track of what was being hauled where, when it was needed, and who would pay for it. The railroad industry reached a historic climax on May 10, 1869, with the completion of the first transcontinental railway. The Union Pacific Railroad, building west from Nebraska, and the Central Pacific Railroad, building east from California, met at Promontory Point, Utah, where a golden spike was driven to set the merging rails. Passenger and freight business on the nation's rail lines peaked in the 1920s and 1930s and then went into decline. Still, rail is an important method of transportation. For example, automobile manufacturers use the railroad more than any other means of transportation to ship completed automobiles. Other commodities, such as coal and farm products, still rely heavily on rail. The railroad system is now a complex, interconnecting network of some 200,000 miles of lines that serve all parts of the country. While computers have eliminated some clerical jobs, clerks are still needed to keep accurate records, compile statistics, and transact railroad business for the complex systems of freight, express, and passenger rail service.

THE JOB

Volumes of paperwork are necessary to keep accurate records and provide information on the business transactions of railroad companies. Railroad clerks are responsible for completing and maintaining this paperwork. They interact with customers of the railroad and railroad employees at all levels.

Traditionally, railroad clerks have been employed in railroad yards, terminals, freight houses, railroad stations, and company offices. However, as railroad companies have merged, and as computerization has increasingly been used, railroads have tended to consolidate much of their operation into a centralized location. As a result, most railroad clerks no longer work on site in the terminals; instead, they work at the railroad's central office. The information they need from the various terminals, yards, and stations is transmitted to them via computer and TV camera.

Clerks may perform a variety of duties, depending on the size of the company they work for and the level of seniority they have achieved. Railroad clerks employed on Class I "line-haul" railroads perform such clerical duties as selling tickets, bookkeeping, compiling statistics, collecting bills, investigating complaints and adjusting claims, and tracing lost or misdirected shipments. *Yard clerks* use information from records or other personnel to prepare orders for railroad yard switching crews. They also keep records of cars moving into or out of the yard.

Pullman car clerks assign and dispatch sleeping cars to railroad companies requesting them and assign Pullman conductors to trains. *Dispatcher clerks* schedule train crews for work, notify them of their assignments, and record the time and distance they work.

Train clerks record the exact time each train arrives at or leaves the station, compare those times with schedules, and inquire about reasons for delays. They also process other data about train movements. *Railroad-maintenance clerks* keep records about repairs being made to tracks or rights-of-way, including the location and type of repair and the materials and time involved.

A great deal of railroad business and income involves moving freight. *Documentation-billing clerks* prepare the billing documents that list a freight shipper's name, the type and weight of cargo, destination, charges, and so on. They total the charges, check for accuracy, and resolve discrepancies. *Demurrage clerks* compute charges for delays in loading or unloading freight, prepare bills for these charges, and send the bills to the shippers or receivers responsible for the delays. They also communicate with shippers and receivers about the time and place of shipment arrival and the time allowed for unloading freight before they levy any charges.

Revising clerks verify and revise freight and tariff charges on shipment bills. *Interline clerks* examine waybills and ticket sales records to compute the charges payable to the various carriers involved in interline business. *Accounts adjustable clerks* compute corrected freight charges from waybill data. *Voucher clerks* receive claims for lost or damaged goods and prorate the cost of the goods to the various carriers involved in an interline shipment. *Express clerks* receive packages from customers, compute charges, write bills, receive payments, issue receipts, and release packages to the proper recipients.

Secretaries, typists, stenographers, bookkeepers, and operators of business and computing machines constitute a second group of railroad clerical workers. All of these employees perform clerical duties that are similar to those performed in other types of business and industry.

Thousands of railroad clerks are employed in higher level jobs that require technical skills and knowledge. Such workers might include *collectors,* who pursue uncollected bills; *accountants,* who are concerned with company financial transactions; and *records and statistical clerks,* responsible for statistical compilations on railroad traffic, employees, and other business details. In addition, these employees are also frequently responsible for compiling periodic reports for the federal government on railroad business, transactions, and operational traffic.

REQUIREMENTS

High School
A high school education is the minimum educational requirement for most railroad clerk positions. You should take business and communications courses, such as English and speech, in high school. Computer science courses are also important.

Postsecondary Training
Students who have postsecondary training in accounting, office management, or computer applications may be in a better position to get

hired as a railroad clerk than students with high school diplomas only. In many instances, companies also require that you successfully pass clerical aptitude tests and be able to type 35–40 words per minute. Finally, because computers are now commonplace in the railroad industry, potential clerks will find that they need a certain degree of computer literacy.

Other Requirements

Patience and attention to detail are important for all clerical workers. Since you may regularly work with the public, a congenial disposition, a pleasant phone voice, and the ability to get along well with others are valuable assets. For example, one major railroad, Norfolk Southern, outlines the following standards for successful candidates for clerk positions: "be responsible and reliable, able to make quick decisions and prioritize work; be energetic and able to handle inquiries with strong interpersonal skills and a customer focus."

EXPLORING

One way to observe the work performed by railroad clerks is to obtain a part-time or summer job with a railroad company as a messenger or office assistant. If a railroad job is not available, working in any sort of office setting might give you experience with clerical work such as typing, stenography, bookkeeping, and the operation of common office equipment.

EMPLOYERS

Railroad clerks may be employed by passenger lines or freight lines. They may work for one of the major railroads, such as Burlington Northern Santa Fe, Norfolk Southern, CSX, or Atchison/Topeka/Santa Fe, or they may work for one of the 500 smaller short line railroads across the country. Clerks who work for a major railroad generally work in a large centralized office with many other workers. Railroad clerks may work in any part of the country, urban or rural. Clerks who are employed by commuter passenger lines work in large metropolitan areas.

STARTING OUT

Railroad companies frequently fill railroad clerical positions by promoting current office assistants, janitors, or messengers. Therefore, you are most likely to find entrance into the field via a lower level job.

Once accepted for employment with a railroad company, you may be given a temporary appointment as an "extra" and listed for "extra board" work until a regular job appointment becomes available.

Individuals interested in railroad clerical jobs may apply directly to the railroad companies or inquire about job application procedures through the union representing this group of employees. Newspaper advertisements may sometimes list openings for clerical employees.

ADVANCEMENT

Seniority plays a key role in advancement within the railroad industry. Jobs with higher pay, better hours, and more responsibility almost always go to those workers who have put in many years with the company. Most clerks are designated trainees for a period of 14–90 days when they first begin working before they advance to full-fledged clerks.

Railroad clerks who have achieved a high level of seniority and who have proven their abilities are sometimes promoted to assistant chief clerks or to positions of higher administrative status. Clerks who continue their formal education and training in some field of specialization, such as accounting or statistics, may have opportunities for promotions into jobs as auditors or statisticians. Other advancement opportunities may include advancement to traffic agent, buyer, storekeeper, or ticket and station agent.

EARNINGS

Salaries for railroad clerks vary depending on union agreements, training, experience, job responsibilities, and the type of operation in which the employee works. In most cases, hourly wages are set by the agreement between the railroad and the union. Clerks represented by the Transportation Communications Union who work for a major railroad start at around $28,500 per year. Those workers on the low end of the pay scale earn between $19,500 and $20,800 annually, while those at the top end can make between $41,600 and $44,200.

The U.S. Department of Labor reports median salaries in 2001 for the following types of clerks: bookkeeping, accounting, and auditing clerks, $26,540; bill and account collectors, $25,960; customer service representatives, $25,430; reservation and transportation ticket agents and travel clerks, $24,090; production, planning, and expediting clerks, $32,420; cargo and freight agents, $30,640; dispatchers,

$30,070; weighers, measurers, checkers, and samplers, recordkeeping, $24,690; and shipping, receiving, and traffic clerks, $22,710.

Railroad employees are usually paid time and a half for any time worked over eight hours a day. Most railroad employees are given paid vacation, sick days, and holidays. Retired railroad workers receive pensions and retirement insurance from the federal Railroad Retirement Administration, which they pay into while they are working.

WORK ENVIRONMENT

A 40-hour workweek is the typical schedule for railroad clerical employees in nonsupervisory positions. Individuals who have temporary appointments may have an irregular work schedule, depending on the type of railroad setting in which they are employed. Clerks are sometimes expected to be available to work in a three-shift operation. Many clerks work strictly during the day, though. The majority of these workers perform their duties in comfortable, well-lit offices or stations. Large company offices may be more elaborately furnished and equipped than those of smaller stations.

The work of railroad clerks is not considered hazardous or physically strenuous; much of it is done while sitting down. Some types of clerical work can be tedious and unexciting, however, and in some cases, they can result in eyestrain. Some clerks have to interact with the public, either by phone or in person. These workers are exposed to various sorts of people, some of whom may be quite difficult.

OUTLOOK

Railroad clerks have been hit hard by the overall decline in railroad business; in the last 15 years, the total number of clerks employed has decreased by 50–60 percent. The increasing use of electronic data processing and computers have also played a large part in the employment decline for these workers, as machines have come to do more and more of the freight bill processing and recording of information on freight movements and yard operations.

Although this decline in employment is expected to continue over the next several years, some job opportunities are expected to become available each year for these workers. Job turnover in this occupational group is relatively high as a result of retirements and employees transferring to other fields.

FOR MORE INFORMATION

For general information on the railroad industry, contact:
Association of American Railroads
50 F Street, NW
Washington, DC 20001-1564
Tel: 202-639-2100
Email: information@aar.org
http://www.aar.org

For information on the career of railroad clerk, contact:
Transportation Communications International Union
3 Research Place
Rockville, MD 20850
Tel: 301-948-4910
http://www.tcunion.org

Receptionists

OVERVIEW

Receptionists—so named because they receive visitors in places of business—have the important job of giving a business's clients and visitors a positive first impression. These front-line workers are the first communication sources who greet clients and visitors, answer their questions, and direct them to the people they wish to see. Receptionists also answer telephones, take and distribute messages for other employees, and make sure no one enters the office unescorted or unauthorized. Many receptionists perform additional clerical duties. *Switchboard operators* perform similar tasks but primarily handle equipment that receives an organization's telephone calls. There are more than 1.1 million receptionists employed throughout the United States.

HISTORY

In the 18th and 19th centuries merchants and other business people began to recognize the importance of giving customers the immediate impression that the business was friendly, efficient, and trustworthy. These businesses began to employ *hosts* and *hostesses*, workers who would greet customers, make them comfortable, and often serve them refreshments while they waited or did business with the owner. As businesses grew larger and more diverse, these hosts and hostesses (only recently renamed receptionists) took on the additional duties of answering phones, keeping track of workers, and directing visitors to the employee they needed to see. Receptionists also began to work as information dispensers, answering growing numbers of inquiries from the public. In the medical field, as services expanded, more receptionists were needed to direct patients to physicians and clinical services and to keep track of appointments and payment information.

Soon receptionists became indispensable to business and service establishments. Today, it is hard to imagine most medium-sized or large businesses functioning without a receptionist.

THE JOB

The receptionist is a specialist in human contact: The most important part of a receptionist's job is dealing with people in a courteous and effective manner. Receptionists greet customers, clients, patients, and salespeople, take their names, and determine the nature of their business and the person they wish to see. The receptionist then pages the requested person, directs the visitor to that person's office or location, or makes an appointment for a later visit. Receptionists often keep records of all visits by writing down the visitor's name, purpose of visit, person visited, and date and time.

Most receptionists answer the telephone at their place of employment; many operate switchboards or paging systems. These workers usually take and distribute messages for other employees and may receive and distribute mail. Receptionists may perform a variety of other clerical duties, including keying in and filing correspondence and other paperwork, proofreading, preparing travel vouchers, and preparing outgoing mail. In some businesses, receptionists are responsible for monitoring the attendance of other employees. In businesses where employees are frequently out of the office on assignments, receptionists may keep track of their whereabouts to ensure they receive important phone calls and messages. Many receptionists use computers and word processors in performing their clerical duties.

Receptionists are partially responsible for maintaining office security, especially in large firms. They may require all visitors to sign in and out and carry visitors' passes during their stay. Since visitors may not enter most offices unescorted, receptionists usually accept and sign for packages and other deliveries.

Receptionists are frequently responsible for answering inquiries from the public about a business's nature and operations. To answer these questions efficiently and in a manner that conveys a favorable impression, a receptionist must be as knowledgeable as possible about the business's products, services, policies, and practices and familiar with the names and responsibilities of all other employees. They must be careful, however, not to divulge classified information such as business procedures or employee activities that a competing company might be able to use. This part of a receptionist's job is so important that some businesses call their receptionists *information clerks*.

A large number of receptionists work in physicians' and dentists' offices, hospitals, clinics, and other health care establishments. Workers in medical offices receive patients, take their names, and escort them to examination rooms. They make future appointments for patients and may prepare statements and collect bill payments. In hospitals, receptionists obtain patient information, assign patients to rooms, and keep records on the dates they are admitted and discharged.

In other types of industries, the duties of these workers vary. Receptionists in hair salons arrange appointments for clients and may escort them to stylists' stations. Workers in bus or train companies answer inquiries about departures, arrivals, and routes. *In-file operators* collect and distribute credit information to clients for credit purposes. *Registrars, park aides,* and *tourist-information assistants* may be employed as receptionists at public or private facilities. Their duties may include keeping a record of the visitors entering and leaving the facility, as well as providing information on services that the facility provides. Information clerks, *automobile club information clerks,* and *referral-and-information aides* provide answers to questions by telephone or in person from both clients and potential clients and keep a record of all inquiries.

Switchboard operators may perform specialized work, such as operating switchboards at police district offices to take calls for assistance from citizens. Or, they may handle airport communication systems, which includes public address paging systems and courtesy telephones, or serve as *answering-service operators*, who record and deliver messages for clients who cannot be reached by telephone.

REQUIREMENTS

High School

You can prepare for a receptionist position by taking courses in business, business math, English, and public speaking. You should also take computer science courses.

Postsecondary Training

Most employees require receptionists to have a high school diploma. Some businesses prefer to hire workers who have completed post-high school courses at a junior college or business school. Courses in basic bookkeeping and principles of accounting helpful. This type of training may lead to a higher-paying receptionist job and a better chance for advancement. Many employers require typing, switchboard, computer, and other clerical skills, but they may provide some on-the-job training as the work is typically entry level.

Medical receptionists make sure patients sign in and complete forms before their medical appointments. *(Corbis)*

Other Requirements

To be a good receptionist, you must be well-groomed, have a pleasant voice, and be able to express yourself clearly. Because you may sometimes deal with demanding people, a smooth, patient disposition and good judgment are important. All receptionists need to be courteous and tactful. A good memory for faces and names also proves very valuable. Most important are good listening and communications skills and an understanding of human nature.

EXPLORING

A good way to obtain experience as a receptionist is through a high school work-study program. Students participating in such programs spend part of their school day in classes and the rest working for local businesses. This arrangement will help you gain valuable practical experience before you look for your first job. High school guidance counselors can provide information about work-study opportunities.

EMPLOYERS

According to the U.S. Department of Labor, approximately 1.1 million people are employed as receptionists, accounting for about a third of all information clerks. Factories, wholesale and retail stores, and service providers employ a large percentage of these workers. Nearly one-third of the receptionists in the United States work in health care settings, including offices, hospitals, nursing homes, urgent care centers, and clinics. Almost one-third work part time.

STARTING OUT

While you are in high school, you may be able to learn of openings with local businesses through your school guidance counselors or newspaper want ads. Local state employment offices frequently have information about receptionist work. You should also contact area businesses for whom you would like to work; many available positions are not advertised in the paper because they are filled so quickly. Temporary-work agencies are a valuable resource for finding jobs.

ADVANCEMENT

Advancement opportunities are limited for receptionists, especially in small offices. The more clerical skills and education workers have, the greater their chances for promotion to such better paying jobs as secretary, administrative assistant, or bookkeeper. College or business school training can help receptionists advance to higher level positions. Many companies provide training for their receptionists and other employees, helping workers gain skills for job advancement.

EARNINGS

Earnings for receptionists vary widely with the education and experience of the worker and type, size, and geographic location of the business. According to an OfficeTeam salary survey, receptionists had starting salaries ranging from $19,500 to $25,000 in 2002. The U.S. Department of Labor reported that in 2001, the median salary for receptionists was $20,650. The lowest-paid 10 percent of these workers made less than $14,280 annually, while the highest paid 10 percent earned more than $30,130 per year. Receptionists are usually eligible for paid holidays and vacations, sick leave, medical and life insurance coverage, and a retirement plan of some kind.

WORK ENVIRONMENT

Receptionists usually work near or at the main entrance to the business. Therefore, these areas are usually pleasant and clean and are carefully furnished and decorated to create a favorable, businesslike impression. Work areas are almost always air-conditioned, well lit, and relatively quiet, although a receptionist's phone rings frequently. Receptionists work behind a desk or counter and spend most of their workday sitting, although some standing and walking is required when filing or escorting visitors to their destinations. The job may be stressful at times, especially when a worker must be polite to rude callers.

Most receptionists work five days, 35–40 hours a week. Some may work weekend and evening hours, especially those in medical offices. Switchboard operators may have to work any shift of the day if their employers require 24-hour phone service, such as hotels and hospitals. These workers usually work holidays and weekend hours.

OUTLOOK

Employment for receptionists is expected to grow faster than the average over the next several years, according to the *Occupational Outlook Handbook*. Many openings will occur due to the occupation's high turnover rate. Opportunities will be best for those with wide clerical skills and work experience. Growth in jobs for receptionists is expected to be greater than for other clerical positions because automation will have little effect on the receptionist's largely interpersonal duties and because of an anticipated growth in the number of businesses providing services. In addition, more and more businesses know how a receptionist can convey a positive public image. Opportunities should be especially good in rapid services industries, such as physician's offices, law firms, temporary help agencies, and consulting firms.

FOR MORE INFORMATION

For information on careers, contact IAAP:
International Association of Administrative Professionals (IAAP)
10502 NW Ambassador Drive
PO Box 20404
Kansas City, MO 64195-0404
Tel: 816-891-6600
Email: service@iaap-hq.org
http://www.iaap-hq.org

Reservation and Ticket Agents

OVERVIEW

Reservation and ticket agents are employed by airlines, bus companies, railroads, and cruise lines to help customers in several ways. *Reservation agents* make and confirm travel arrangements for passengers by using computers and manuals to determine timetables, taxes, and other information. *Ticket agents* sell tickets in terminals or in separate offices. Like reservation agents, they also use computers and manuals containing scheduling, boarding, and rate information to plan routes and calculate ticket costs. They determine whether seating is available, answer customer inquiries, check baggage, and direct passengers to proper places for boarding. They may also announce arrivals and departures and assist passengers in boarding. There are approximately 191,000 reservation and ticket agents employed in the United States.

HISTORY

Since the earliest days of commercial passenger transportation (by boat or stagecoach), someone has been responsible for making sure that space is available and that everyone on board pays the proper fare. As transportation grew into a major industry over the years, the job of making reservations and selling tickets became a specialized occupation.

The airline industry experienced its first boom in the early 1930s. By the end of that decade, millions of people were flying each year. Since the introduction of passenger-carrying jet planes in 1958, the

QUICK FACTS

School Subjects
Business
Computer science
English

Personal Skills
Communication/ideas
Helping/teaching

Work Environment
Primarily indoors
Primarily one location

Minimum Education Level
Some postsecondary training

Salary Range
$16,330 to $24,090 to
$44,150+

Certification or Licensing
None available

Outlook
About as fast as the average

DOT
238

GOE
07.03.01

NOC
6433

O*NET-SOC
43-4181.00, 43-4181.01,
43-4181.02

number of people traveling by air has multiplied many times over. Airlines now employ about six out of every 10 reservation and ticket agents.

A number of innovations have helped make the work of reservation and ticket agents easier and more efficient. The introduction of automated telephone services allows customers to check on flight availability and arrival/departure times without having to wait to speak to an agent. Computers have both simplified the agents' work and put more resources within their reach. Since the 1950s, many airlines have operated computerized scheduling and reservation systems, either individually or in partnership with other airlines. Until recently, these systems were not available to the general consumer. In the last decade, however, the growth of the Internet has permitted travelers to access scheduling and rate information, make reservations, and purchase tickets without contacting an agent. Airlines now offer electronic tickets, which they expect will eventually replace the traditional paper ticket. Despite these innovations, there will always be a need for reservation and ticketing agents, primarily for safety and security purposes. These employees still fill a vital role in the transportation industry.

THE JOB

Airline reservation agents are sales agents who work in large central offices run by airline companies. Their primary job is to book and confirm reservations for passengers on scheduled flights. At the request of the customer or a ticket agent, they plan the itinerary and other travel arrangements. While many agents still use timetables, airline manuals, reference guides, and tariff books, most of this work is performed using specialized computer programs.

Computers are used to make, confirm, change, and cancel reservations. After asking for the passenger's destination, desired travel time, and airport of departure, reservation agents type the information into a computer and quickly obtain information on all flight schedules and seating availability. If the plane is full, the agent may suggest an alternative flight or check to see if space is available on another airline that flies to the same destination. Agents may even book seats on competing airlines, especially if their own airline can provide service on the return trip.

Reservation agents also answer telephone inquiries about such things as schedules, fares, arrival and departure times, and cities serviced by their airline. They may maintain an inventory of passenger space available so they can notify other personnel and ticket stations of changes and try to book all flights to capacity. Some reservation

Two airline agents check a passenger's identification before she heads off to her gate. *(Corbis)*

agents work in more specialized areas, handling calls from travel agents or booking flights for members of frequent flyer programs. Agents working with international airlines must also be informed of visa regulations and other travel developments. The *senior reservation agent,* who supervises and coordinates the activities of the other agents, usually supplies this information.

In the railroad industry, *train reservation clerks* perform tasks similar to those just mentioned. They book seats or compartments for passengers, keep station agents and clerks advised on available space, and communicate with reservation clerks in other towns.

General transportation ticket agents for any mode of travel (air, bus, rail, or ship) sell tickets to customers at terminals or at separate ticket offices. Like reservation agents, they book space for customers. In addition, they use computers to prepare and print tickets, calculate fares, and collect payment. At the terminals they check and tag luggage, direct passengers to the proper areas for boarding, keep records of passengers on each departure, and help with customer problems, such as lost baggage or missed connections. Airline ticket agents may have additional duties, such as paging arriving and departing passengers and finding accommodations or new travel arrangements for passengers in the event of flight cancellations.

In airports, *gate agents* assign seats, issue boarding passes, make public address announcements of departures and arrivals, and help elderly or disabled passengers board the planes. In addition, they may also provide information to disembarking passengers about ground transportation, connecting flights, and local hotels.

Regardless of where they work, reservation and transportation ticket agents must be knowledgeable about their companies' policies and procedures, as well as the standard procedures of their industry. They must be aware of the availability of special promotions and services and be able to answer any questions customers may have.

REQUIREMENTS

High School

Reservation and ticket agents are generally required to have at least a high school diploma. Applicants should be able to type and have good communication and problem-solving skills. Because computers are being used more and more in this field, you should have a basic knowledge of computers and computer software. Previous experience working with the public is also helpful for the job. Knowledge of geography and foreign languages are other valuable skills, especially for international service agents.

Postsecondary Training

Some college education is preferred for these positions, although it is not considered essential for the job. Some colleges now offer courses specifically designed for ticket reservations.

Reservation agents are given about a month of classroom instruction. Here you will be taught how to read schedules, calculate fares, and plan itineraries. They learn how to use computer programs to get information and reserve space efficiently. They also study company policies and government regulations that apply to the industry.

Transportation ticket agents receive less training, consisting of about one week of classroom instruction. They learn how to read tickets and schedules, assign seats, and tag baggage. This is followed by one week of on-the-job training, working alongside an experienced agent. After mastering the simpler tasks, the new ticket agents are trained to reserve space, make out tickets, and handle the boarding gate.

Other Requirements

Because you will be in constant contact with the public, professional appearance, a clear and pleasant speaking voice, and a friendly personality are important qualities. You need to be tactful in keeping telephone time to a minimum without alienating your customers. In addition, you should enjoy working with people, have a good memory, and be able to maintain your composure when working with harried or unhappy travelers. Agents form a large part of the public image of their company.

Although not a requirement, many agents belong to labor unions, such as the Air Line Employees Association, the Transport Workers Union of America, and the International Brotherhood of Teamsters.

EXPLORING

In order to get a feel for this type of career, you may wish to apply for part-time or summer work with transportation companies in their central offices or at terminals. A school counselor can help you arrange an information interview with an experienced reservation and transportation ticket agent. Talking to an agent directly about his or her duties can help you to become more familiar with transportation operations.

EMPLOYERS

Reservation and ticket agents hold approximately 191,000 jobs in the United States. Commercial airlines are the main employers. However, other transportation companies, such as rail, ship, and bus lines, also require their services.

STARTING OUT

To find part-time or summer work, apply directly to the personnel or employment offices of transportation companies. Ask your school counselor or college placement director for information about job openings, requirements, and possible training programs. Additionally, contact transportation unions for lists of job openings.

ADVANCEMENT

With experience and a good work record, some reservation and ticket agents can be promoted to supervisory positions. They can also become city and district sales managers for ticket offices. Beyond this, opportunities for advancement are limited. However, achieving seniority within a company can give an agent the first choice of shifts and available overtime.

EARNINGS

According to the U.S. Department of Labor, reservation and transportation ticket agents earned median salaries of approximately $24,090 in 2001. The lowest-paid 10 percent of these workers made less than $16,330 per year, while the highest-paid 10 percent earned more than $44,150 annually.

Most agents can earn overtime pay; many employers also pay extra for night work. Benefits vary according to the place of work, experience, and union membership; however, most receive vacation and sick pay, health insurance, and retirement plans. Agents, especially those employed by the airlines, often receive free or reduced-fare transportation for themselves and their families.

WORK ENVIRONMENT

Reservation and ticket agents generally work 40 hours per week. Those working in reservations typically work in cubicles with their own computer terminals and telephone headsets. They are often on the telephone and behind their computers all day long. Conversations with customers and computer activity may be monitored and recorded by their supervisors for evaluation and quality reasons. Agents might also be required to achieve sales or reservations quotas. During holidays or when special promotions and discounts are being offered, agents are especially busy. At these times or during periods of severe weather, passengers may become difficult. Handling customer frustrations can be stressful, but agents must maintain composure and a pleasant manner when speaking with customers.

Ticket agents working in airports and train and bus stations face a busy and noisy environment. They may stand most of the day and lift heavy objects such as luggage and packages. During holidays and busy times, their work can become extremely hectic as they process long lines of waiting customers. Storms and other factors may delay or even cancel flights, trains, and bus services. Like reservation agents, ticket agents may be confronted with upset passengers, but must be able to maintain composure at all times.

OUTLOOK

According to the U.S. Department of Labor, employment for reservation and ticket agents is expected to grow about as fast as the average for all occupations over the next several years. Technology is changing the way consumers purchase tickets. "Ticketless" travel, or automated reservations ticketing, is reducing the need for agents. In addition, many airports now have computerized kiosks that allow passengers to reserve and purchase tickets themselves. Passengers can also access information about fares and flight times on the Internet, where they can also make reservations and purchase tickets. However, for security reasons, all of these services cannot be fully automated, so the need for reservation and transportation ticket agents will never be completely eliminated.

Most openings will occur as experienced agents transfer to other occupations or retire. Competition for jobs is fierce due to declining demand, low turnover, and because of the glamour and attractive travel benefits associated with the industry.

Overall, the transportation industry will remain heavily dependent on the state of the economy. During periods of recession or public fear about the safety of air travel, passenger travel generally declines and transportation companies are less likely to hire new workers, or may even resort to layoffs. The terrorist attacks that took place in September 2001 have greatly affected the transportation industry. In the short term, the general public feared traveling far from home, especially by air, because of threats of further attacks. However, the World Tourism Organization (WTO) predicts that the industry will rebound in the long term. The economic need for business travel—as well as the public's desire for personal travel—will not be permanently altered by external events, states the WTO.

FOR MORE INFORMATION

For information on the airline industry, contact the FAA.
Federal Aviation Administration (FAA)
800 Independence Avenue, SW, Room 810
Washington, DC 20591
Tel: 202-366-4000
http://www.faa.gov

For information on education, internships, scholarships, or certification in travel and tourism, contact:
National Tourism Foundation
546 East Main Street
PO Box 3071
Lexington, KY 40508
Tel: 800-682-8886
Email: ntf@ntastaff.com
http://www.ntfonline.com

For statistics on international travel and tourism, visit the following website:

World Tourism Organization
Capitán Haya 42
28020 Madrid, Spain
Email: omt@world-tourism.org
http://www.world-tourism.org

Secretaries

OVERVIEW

Secretaries, or *administrative assistants,* perform a wide range of jobs that vary greatly from business to business. However, most secretaries key in documents, manage records and information, answer telephones, handle correspondence, schedule appointments, make travel arrangements, and sort mail. The amount of time secretaries spend on these duties depends on the size and type of the office as well as on their own job training. There are approximately 3.9 million secretaries employed in the United States.

HISTORY

People have always needed to communicate with one another for societies to function efficiently. Today, as in the past, secretaries play an important role in keeping lines of communication open. Before there were telephones, messages were transmitted by hand, often from the secretary of one party to the secretary of the receiving party. Their trustworthiness was valued because the lives of many people often hung in the balance of certain communications.

Secretaries in the ancient world developed methods of taking abbreviated notes so that they could capture as much as possible of their employers' words. The modern precursors of the shorthand methods we know today developed in 16th-century England. In the 19th century, Isaac Pitman and John Robert Gregg developed the shorthand systems that are still used in offices and courtrooms in the United States.

The equipment secretaries use in their work has changed drastically in recent years. Almost every office, from the smallest to the largest,

QUICK FACTS

School Subjects
Business
Computer science
English

Personal Skills
Communication/ideas
Following instructions

Work Environment
Primarily indoors
Primarily one location

Minimum Education Level
High school diploma

Salary Range
$15,550 to $24,640 to
   $53,280+

Certification or Licensing
Voluntary

Outlook
Little change or more slowly
   than the average

DOT
201

GOE
07.01.03

NOC
1241

O*NET-SOC
43-6012.00, 43-6013.00,
   43-6014.00

is automated in some way. Familiarity with machines including switchboards, Dictaphones, photocopiers, fax machines, and personal computers has become an integral part of the secretary's day-to-day work.

THE JOB

Secretaries perform a variety of administrative and clerical duties. The goal of all their activities is to assist their employers in the execution of their work and to help their companies conduct business in an efficient and professional manner.

Secretaries' work includes processing and transmitting information to the office staff and to other organizations. They operate office machines and arrange for their repair or servicing. These machines include computers, typewriters, dictating machines, photocopiers, switchboards, and fax machines. These secretaries also order office supplies and perform regular duties such as answering phones, sorting mail, managing files, taking dictation, and composing and keying in letters.

Some offices have word processing centers that handle all of the firm's typing. In such a situation, *administrative secretaries* take care of all secretarial duties except for typing and dictation. This arrangement leaves them free to respond to correspondence, prepare reports, do research and present the results to their employers, and otherwise assist the professional staff. Often these secretaries work in groups of three or four so that they can help each other if one secretary has a workload that is heavier than normal.

In many offices, secretaries make appointments for company executives and keep track of the office schedule. They make travel arrangements for the professional staff or for clients, and occasionally are asked to travel with staff members on business trips. Other secretaries might manage the office while their supervisors are away on vacation or business trips.

Secretaries take minutes at meetings, write up reports, and compose and type letters. They often will find their responsibilities growing as they learn the business. Some are responsible for finding speakers for conferences, planning receptions, and arranging public relations programs. Some write copy for brochures or articles before making the arrangements to have them printed or microfilmed, or they might use desktop publishing software to create the documents themselves. They greet clients and guide them to the proper offices, and they often supervise and train other staff members and newer secretaries, especially in computer software programs.

Some secretaries perform very specialized work. Legal secretaries prepare legal papers including wills, mortgages, contracts, deeds, motions, complaints, and summonses. They work under the direct supervision of an attorney or paralegal. They assist with legal research by reviewing legal journals and organizing briefs for their employers. They must learn an entire specialized vocabulary that is used in legal papers and documents. For more information on this career, see the article "Legal Secretaries."

Medical secretaries take medical histories of patients, make appointments, prepare and send bills to patients (as well as track and collect them), process insurance billing, maintain medical files, and pursue correspondence with patients, hospitals, and associations. They assist physicians or medical scientists with articles, reports, speeches, and conference proceedings. Some medical secretaries are responsible for ordering medical supplies. They, too, need to learn an entire specialized vocabulary of medical terms and be familiar with laboratory or hospital procedures. For more information on this career, see the article "Medical Secretaries."

Technical secretaries work for engineers and scientists. They prepare reports and papers that often include graphics and mathematical equations that are difficult to format on paper. The secretaries maintain a technical library and help with scientific papers by gathering and editing materials.

Social secretaries, often called *personal secretaries*, arrange all of the social activities of their employers. They handle private as well as business social affairs, and they may plan parties, send out invitations, or write speeches for their employers. Social secretaries often work for celebrities or high-level executives who have busy social calendars to maintain.

Many associations, clubs, and nonprofit organizations have *membership secretaries* who compile and send out newsletters or promotional materials while maintaining membership lists, dues records, and directories. Depending on the type of club, the secretary may be the one who gives out information to prospective members and who keeps current members and related organizations informed of upcoming events.

Education secretaries work in elementary or secondary schools or on college campuses. They take care of all clerical duties at the school. Their responsibilities may include preparing bulletins and reports for teachers, parents, or students, keeping track of budgets for school supplies or student activities, and maintaining the school's calendar of events. Depending on the position, they may work for school administrators, principals, or groups of teachers or professors. Other

A secretary works with her supervisor as he signs a document. *(Corbis)*

education secretaries work in administration offices, state education departments, or service departments.

REQUIREMENTS

High School

You will need at least a high school diploma to enter this field. To prepare for a career as a secretary, take high school courses including business, English, and speech. Keyboarding and computer science courses will also be helpful.

Postsecondary Training

To succeed as a secretary, you will need good office skills that include rapid and accurate keyboarding skills and good spelling and grammar. You should enjoy handling details. Some positions require typing a minimum number of words per minute, as well as shorthand ability. Knowledge of word processing, spreadsheets, and database management is important, and many employers require it. You can learn some of these skills in business education courses taught at vocational and business schools.

Certification or Licensing

Qualifying for the designation Certified Professional Secretary (CPS) rating is increasingly recognized in business and industry as a consideration for promotion as a senior level secretary. The International Association of Administrative Professionals administers the examinations required for this certification. Secretaries with limited experience can become an Accredited Legal Secretary (ALS) by obtaining certification from the Certifying Board of the National Association of Legal Secretaries. Those with at least three years of experience in the legal field can be certified as a Professional Legal Secretary (PLS) from this same organization. Legal Secretaries International offers the Certified Legal Secretary Specialist designation in four categories: business law, civil trial, probate, and real estate.

Other Requirements

Personal qualities are important in this field of work. As a secretary, you will often be the first employee of a company that clients meet, and therefore you must be friendly, poised, and professionally dressed. Because you must work closely with others, you should be personable and tactful. Discretion, good judgment, organizational ability, and initiative are also important. These traits will not only get you hired but will also help you advance in your career.

Some employers encourage their secretaries to take advanced courses and to be trained to use any new piece of equipment in the office. Requirements vary widely from company to company.

EXPLORING

High school guidance counselors can give interest and aptitude tests to help you assess your suitability for a career as a secretary. Local business schools often welcome visitors, and sometimes offer courses that can be taken in conjunction with a high school business course. Work-study programs will also provide you with an opportunity to work in a business setting to get a sense of the work performed by secretaries.

Part-time or summer jobs as receptionists, file clerks, and office clerks are often available in various offices. These jobs are the best indicators of future satisfaction in the secretarial field. You may find a part-time job if you are computer literate. Cooperative education programs arranged through schools and "temping" through an agency also are valuable ways to acquire experience. In general, any job that teaches basic office skills is helpful.

EMPLOYERS

There are 3.9 million secretaries employed throughout the United States, making this profession one of the largest in the country. Of this total, 279,000 specialize as legal secretaries and 314,000 work as medical secretaries. Secretaries are employed in almost every type of industry. Approximately 60 percent of secretaries work in the legal, education, health, and business industries. Others work in banking, financial services, real estate, construction, manufacturing, transportation, communications, and retail and wholesale trade. A large number of secretaries are employed by federal, state, and local government offices.

STARTING OUT

Most people looking for work as secretaries find jobs through the newspaper ads or by applying directly to local businesses. Both private employment offices and state employment services place secretaries, and business schools help their graduates find suitable jobs. Temporary-help agencies are an excellent way to find secretarial jobs, many of which may turn into permanent ones.

ADVANCEMENT

Secretaries often begin by assisting executive secretaries and work their way up by learning the way their business operates. Initial promotions from a secretarial position are usually to jobs such as secretarial supervisor, office manager, or administrative assistant. Depending on other personal qualifications, college courses in business, accounting, or marketing can help the ambitious secretary enter middle and upper management. Training in computer skills can also lead to advancement. Secretaries who become proficient in word processing, for instance, can get jobs as instructors or as sales representatives for software manufacturers.

Many legal secretaries, with additional training and schooling, become paralegals. Secretaries in the medical field can advance into the fields of radiological and surgical records or medical transcription.

EARNINGS

Salaries for secretaries vary widely by region, type of business, and the skill, experience, and level of responsibility of the secretary. Secretaries (except legal, medical, and executive) earned an average of $24,640 annually in 2001, according to the U.S. Department of Labor. Salaries for these workers ranged from a low of $15,550 to a high of more than $37,450. Secretaries employed by the federal government earned a starting salary of $17,474 a year in 2001; secretaries with more experience started at $33,354.

Medical secretaries earned salaries that ranged from less than $17,650 to $36,520 or more per year in 2001, according to the Department of Labor. Legal secretaries made an average of $34,610 in 2001. Salaries for legal secretaries ranged from $22,360 to more than $53,280 annually. An attorney's rank in the firm will also affect the earnings of a legal secretary; secretaries who work for a partner will earn higher salaries than those who work for an associate.

Secretaries, especially those working in the legal profession, earn considerably more if certified. Most secretaries receive paid holidays and two weeks vacation after a year of work, as well as sick leave. Many offices provide benefits including health and life insurance, pension plans, overtime pay, and tuition reimbursement.

WORK ENVIRONMENT

Most secretaries work in pleasant offices with modern equipment. Office conditions vary widely, however. While some secretaries have their own offices and work for one or two executives, others share crowded workspace with other workers.

Most office workers work 35–40 hours a week. Very few secretaries work on the weekends on a regular basis, although some may be asked to work overtime if a particular project demands it.

The work is not physically strenuous or hazardous, although deadline pressure is a factor and sitting for long periods of time can be uncomfortable. Many hours spent in front of a computer can lead to eyestrain or repetitive-motion problems for secretaries. Most secretaries are not required to travel. Part-time and flexible schedules are easily adaptable to secretarial work.

OUTLOOK

The U.S. Department of Labor predicts that employment for secretaries who specialize in legal or medical fields, or who work as executive secretaries, will grow about as fast as the average over the next several years. Those secretaries who do not specialize can expect slower than average job opportunities. Industries such as computer and data processing, engineering and management, and personnel supply will create the most new job opportunities. As common with large occupations, the need to replace retiring workers will generate many openings.

Computers, fax machines, electronic mail, copy machines, and scanners are some technological advancements that have greatly improved the work productivity of secretaries. Company downsizing and restructuring, in some cases, have redistributed traditional secretarial duties to other employees. There has been a growing trend in assigning one secretary to assist two or more managers, adding to this field's decline. Though more professionals are using personal computers for their correspondence, some administrative duties will still need to be handled by secretaries. The personal aspects of the job and responsibilities such as making travel arrangements, scheduling conferences, and transmitting staff instructions have not changed.

Many employers currently complain of a shortage of capable secretaries. Those with skills and experience will have the best chances for employment. Specialized secretaries should attain certification in their field to stay competitive.

FOR MORE INFORMATION

For general career information, contact:
Association of Business Support Services International
5852 Oak Meadow Drive
Yorba Linda, CA 92886-5930
Tel: 714-695-9398
Email: info@abssi.org
http://www.abssi.org

For information on the Certified Professional Secretary Designation, contact:
International Association of Administrative Professionals
10502 NW Ambassador Drive
PO Box 20404
Kansas City, MO 64195-0404
Tel: 816-891-6600

Email: service@iaap-hq.org
http://www.iaap-hq.org

For information about certification, contact:
Legal Secretaries International, Inc.
4301 Windfern Road
Houston, TX 77041-8915
http://www.legalsecretaries.org

For information on the Certified Professional Legal Secretary and the Accredited Legal Secretary designations, contact:
National Association of Legal Secretaries
314 East 3rd Street, Suite 210
Tulsa, OK 74120-2409
Tel: 918-582-5188
Email: info@nals.org
http://www.nals.org

For information regarding union representation, contact:
Office and Professional Employees International Union
265 West 14th Street, Sixth Floor
New York, NY 10011
Tel: 800-346-7348
http://www.opeiu.org

For employment information, contact:
OfficeTeam
2884 Sand Hill Road
Menlo Park, CA 94025
Tel: 800-804-8367
http://www.officeteam.com

The Mayo Clinic is a major employer of medical secretaries. Visit their website for more information:
Mayo Clinic
http://www.mayo.edu

INTERVIEW

Randy Johnson has been an administrative assistant in the Chicago-land area for over 15 years. Johnson spoke with the editors of Careers in Focus: Clerks & Administrative Workers *about his career.*

Q. Please briefly describe your primary and secondary job duties.

A. The workload of an office assistant is so varied, that I'd have to say that the primary job duty is to please your employer. The secondary responsibility is to achieve self-satisfaction in a job well done.

Q. Where do you work, indoors or outdoors? Do you travel for your job?

A. There is no indoor/outdoor option with this position; one must decide if they would prefer to work in a small, informal family company environment; or, you may decide to work for a large, international conglomerate. Travel opportunities will depend upon your responsibilities and expertise and the size and demands of your employer.

Q. How did you train for this job? What was your college major?

A. I received my education and initial experience in the military. During wartime, I decided that training for an office environment would keep me off the frontlines and provide me with skills that I would benefit from when I would return to civilian life. I received the rest of my training while on the job.

Q. Did you participate in any internships while you were in college?

A. I started my career during simpler times: As long as you knew how to type, you could get a job anywhere. Keeping and progressing in the job required continuing education. Today, knowing how to type isn't enough to secure an assistant's position: You are expected to be able to use a number of computer programs.

Q. How/where did you get your first job in this field? What did you do?

A. I found my first office position through an employment service. I stayed with the firm for 15 years. I got very good at all that I did—it took three people to replace me when I left. It wasn't unusual for me to have two or even three printers working at the same time while I had the photocopier going, and I'd also be on the telephone trying to calm an upset customer.

Q. What kind of sources are available to someone looking to get into this field?

A. It has always been easy to find a position as an administrative assistant. There is always a growing firm that realizes they will need [more] help in order to grow and expand. Employment services, word-or-mouth, and the Internet are all good sources to locate a position.

Q. What are the most important personal and professional qualities for people in your career?
A. Personality and interpersonal skills are what will put you over the top in a job interview. Everyone can type, everyone can file, everyone can keep the office organized; your potential employer is looking for a friendly disposition—someone who is a joy to work with. Once you have your position, you must continue to prove your worth on a daily basis.

Q. What are some of the pros and cons of your job?
A. This is a "power behind the throne" position. It is unlikely that you will be promoted to management. . . . Your greatest source of job satisfaction will be the pride that you take in your job performance.

Statistical Clerks

QUICK FACTS

School Subjects
Business
Computer science
Mathematics

Personal Skills
Following instructions
Technical/scientific

Work Environment
Primarily indoors
Primarily one location

Minimum Education Level
High school diploma

Salary Range
$15,000 to $28,990 to
$43,940+

Certification or Licensing
None available

Outlook
Little change or more slowly
than the average

DOT
216

GOE
07.02.03

NOC
1454

O*NET-SOC
43-9111.00

OVERVIEW

Statistical clerks perform routine tasks associated with data collection, data file management, data entry, and data processing. They work in a number of different industries, including advertising, insurance, manufacturing, and health care, compiling and managing information. There are approximately 25,800 statistical clerks employed in the United States.

HISTORY

According to the earliest records, the study of mathematics was developed to meet the practical business needs of farmers and merchants between 3000 and 2000 B.C. in Egypt and Mesopotamia. One branch of applied mathematics, statistics, deals with the collection and classification of various data by certain numerical characteristics. This information is then used to make inferences and predictions in related situations. A relatively young discipline, statistics emerged in 1892 with the publication of *The Grammar of Science*. Its author, Karl Pearson, a mathematics professor at the University of London, is generally regarded as the father of statistics.

Statistics is widely used by many types of businesses today. Insurance companies use statistics to determine the probability of accidents and deaths in order to set reasonable premium rates for their policyholders. Statistics is used to determine the audience ratings of television shows and approval ratings of politicians. It can be used in disease prevention and economic projections. As business decisions increasingly depend on demographics and other information that can be tabulated, statistical clerks will continue to play a role in the compilation of relevant data.

THE JOB

Statistical clerks are involved in record-keeping and data retrieval. They compile numerical information (questionnaire results and production records, for example) and tabulate it using statistical formulas so that it can be used for further study. They also perform data entry and data processing on computers and are responsible for quality control of the collected data. With the advanced statistical software programs now available, almost all statistical clerks use computers in their work. They also perform clerical functions, such as filing and file management.

Statistical clerks work in a number of fields in a variety of jobs. *Compilers* analyze raw data gathered from surveys, census data, and other reports and organize them into specified categories or groupings. These statistics are compiled into survey findings or census reports. Compilers may prepare graphs or charts to illustrate their findings.

Advertising statistical clerks tabulate statistical records for companies on the cost, volume, and effectiveness of the companies' advertising. They often compare the amount of their customers' merchandise that is sold before an advertising campaign to the amount sold after the campaign to determine whether the campaign influenced consumer behavior.

Medical record clerks and technicians tabulate statistics to be used by medical researchers. They also compile, verify, and file the medical records of hospital or clinic patients and make sure that these records are complete and up to date. Medical record technicians may also assist in compiling the necessary information used in completing hospital insurance billing forms.

Chart calculators work for power companies. They record the net amount of electric power used by the company's customers to check that the correct rates are being charged. They enter power usage information on record forms so that customers are billed at the appropriate rates. *Chart clerks* compile records measuring the quantity of natural or manufactured gas produced, transported, and sold to calculate the volume of gas and petroleum that flows through specific pipelines.

Planimeter operators use a special measuring tool to trace the boundaries of specified land areas. They usually use aerial photographs to help identify the boundary lines of individual plots of land.

Chart changers record data from instruments that measure industrial processes. They are also responsible for maintaining these recording instruments, such as pyrometers and flowmeters.

Actuarial clerks compile data on insurance policies, rates, and claims so that insurance commissioners and companies know how to set their rates.

REQUIREMENTS

High School
A high school diploma is usually sufficient for beginning statistical clerks. High school students should take courses in English, mathematics, and science, as well as business-related courses such as keyboarding and bookkeeping. Because computers are so commonly used in this career, it is important to take as many basic computer courses as you can.

Postsecondary Training
Many community colleges and vocational schools offer business education courses that provide additional training for statistical clerks in the areas of data processing and office procedures. Taking additional computer classes to learn word processing, database, and spreadsheet programs will also be very helpful. As in most career fields, clerks who have obtained further education and have proven their capabilities typically have more advancement opportunities.

Other Requirements
Prospective clerks need to have some mechanical aptitude to be able to operate computers and other office equipment. The ability to concentrate for long periods of time on sometimes repetitive tasks is also important. You should find systematic and orderly work appealing and enjoy working on detailed tasks. In addition, you should work well both independently and with others.

EXPLORING

If you are interested in a career as a statistical clerk, you might gain related experience by taking on clerical or bookkeeping responsibilities with a school club or other organization. In addition, some work-study programs may offer partnerships with businesses for part-time, on-the-job training. Another way to find a part-time or summer job in a business office is by contacting offices directly.

To learn how to operate business machinery and computer software programs, you might consider taking an evening course offered by a local business school or community college. There you might establish business contacts in your classroom, either through other students or through your teacher. To gain insight into the responsi-

Statistical Questions by Industry

- **Government:** How many people are unemployed this month?

- **Environment:** How has the spread of pollution affected a certain area?

- **Market Research:** What are the demographics of certain television viewers?

- **Medicine:** What results has a new medical treatment provided in the past year?

- **Psychology:** Which personality types have found the most success in human resources careers?

- **Population research:** What trends in population growth have developed in China in recent years?

- **Geography:** What does geographical data suggest will happen to the world's remaining glaciers?

- **Sociology:** Which socioeconomic classes perform the best in college?

bilities of a statistical clerk, talk to someone already working in the field about the job and how he or she got started.

EMPLOYERS

In general, statistical clerks are employed by the same sorts of employers that hire statisticians. The federal government hires statisticians in such areas as the Departments of Commerce, Health and Human Services, and Agriculture. Various sectors of private industry also hire both statisticians and statistical clerks. Private-industry employers include insurance companies, utility research and testing services, management and public relations firms, computer and data processing firms, manufacturing companies, and financial services firms. Other statistical clerks may work for researchers in colleges or universities. Approximately 25,800 statistical clerks are employed in the United States.

STARTING OUT

When looking for an entry-level statistical clerk's job, you might first scan the help wanted sections of area newspapers. You can also contact the personnel or human resources offices of businesses or government agencies directly.

Most companies provide on-the-job training for entry-level statistical clerks; during training the company policies and procedures are explained. Beginning clerks work with experienced personnel during this period.

ADVANCEMENT

In many instances, statistical clerks begin their employment as general office clerks and become statistical clerks only after further experience and training. With experience, they may receive more complicated assignments and assume a greater responsibility for the total statistical work to be completed. Those with leadership skills may become group managers or supervisors. In order to become an accountant or bookkeeper, it is usually necessary to get a degree or have other specialized training.

The high turnover rate in this profession increases opportunities for promotion. The number and kinds of opportunities, however, may depend on the place of employment and the ability, training, and experience of the employee.

EARNINGS

Statistical clerks' earnings are similar to those of data-entry clerks. Although salaries vary depending on skill, experience, level of responsibility, and geographic location, a newly hired, inexperienced statistical clerk might expect to earn between $15,000 and $20,000 annually. Statistical clerks earned a median hourly salary of $13.94 in 2001, according to the U.S. Department of Labor. The highest 10 percent earned $43,940 or more in 2001. Fringe benefits for full-time workers include paid vacations, health insurance, and other benefits.

WORK ENVIRONMENT

Statistical clerks work an average of 40 hours per week, usually in a well-ventilated and well-lighted office. Although statistical clerks perform a variety of tasks, the job itself can be fairly routine and repetitive. Statistical clerks who work at video display terminals for long periods of time may experience some eye and neck strain. Clerks often interact with accountants and other office personnel and may work under close supervision.

OUTLOOK

According to the U.S. Department of Labor, little or no employment change is expected for statistical clerks over the next several years. This is a result of new data processing equipment that can now do many of the record-keeping and data-retrieval functions previously performed by statistical clerks. Despite this prediction, however, job openings in this career will arise due to people retiring from or leaving the field. Opportunities should be especially good for those with training in computers and other types of automated office machinery.

FOR MORE INFORMATION

For information on careers in statistics or schools that offer degrees in statistics, contact:
American Statistical Association
1429 Duke Street
Alexandria, VA 22314-3415
Tel: 888-231-3473
http://www.amstat.org

For information on schools and career opportunities in statistics in Canada, contact:
Statistical Society of Canada
1485 Laperrière Street
Ottawa, ON K1Z 7S8 Canada
Tel: 613-725-2253
Email: info@ssc.ca
http://www.ssc.ca

Stenographers

OVERVIEW

Stenographers take dictation using either shorthand notation or a stenotype machine, then later transcribe their notes into business documents. They may record people's remarks at meetings or other proceedings and later give a summary report or a word-for-word transcript of what was said. General stenographers may also perform other office tasks such as typing, filing, answering phones, and operating office machines.

HISTORY

Because of the need for accurate records of speeches, meetings, legal proceedings, and other events, people throughout history have experimented with methods and symbols for abbreviating spoken communications. Contemporary shorthand systems are based on the phonetic principle of using a symbol to represent a sound. Stenographers use a special keyboard called a steno keyboard or shorthand machine to "write" what they hear as they hear it.

Shorthand began to be applied to business communications with the invention of the typewriter. The stenotype, the first machine that could print shorthand characters, was invented in 1910. Unlike a traditional typewriter keyboard, the steno keyboard allows more than one key to be pressed at a time. Although the basic concept behind machine shorthand is phonetic, where combinations of keys represent sounds, the actual theory used is much more complex than straight phonetics.

Today, stenographers, in addition to using stenotype machines, may use Dictaphones or computer-based systems to transcribe reports, letters, and official records of meetings or other events. Their careful and accurate work is essential to the proper functioning of various organizations of law, business, and government.

THE JOB

Stenographers take dictation and then transcribe their notes on a typewriter or word processor. They may be asked to record speeches, conversations, legal proceedings, meetings, or a person's business correspondence. They may either take shorthand manually or use a stenotype machine.

In addition to transcription tasks, general stenographers may also have a variety of other office duties, such as typing, operating photocopy and other office machines, answering telephones, and performing general receptionist duties. They may sit in on staff meetings and later transcribe a summary report of the proceedings for use by management. In some situations, stenographers may be responsible for answering routine office mail.

Experienced and highly skilled stenographers take on more difficult dictation assignments. They may take dictation in foreign languages or at very busy proceedings. Some work as *public stenographers,* who are hired out to serve traveling business people and unique meetings and events.

Steno pool supervisors supervise and coordinate the work of stenographers by assigning them to people who have documents to dictate or by giving stenographers manuscripts, spools of tape, or recordings to transcribe. They also check final typed copy for accuracy.

Skilled stenographers who receive additional training may learn to operate computer-aided transcription (CAT) systems—stenotype machines that are linked directly to a computer. Specialized computer software instantly translates stenographic symbols into words. This technology is most frequently used by real-time captioners or others doing computer-aided real-time translation in courtrooms, classrooms, or meetings, and it requires a more sophisticated knowledge of computer systems and English grammar, along with enhanced technical skills. Other areas of specialization for stenographers include the following:

- *Print shop stenographers* take dictation and operate a special typewriter that produces metal printing plates for use by addressing machines.

- *Transcribing-machine operators* listen to recordings (often through earphones or earplugs) and use a typewriter or word processor to transcribe the material. They can control the speed of the tape so that they can type every word they hear at a comfortable speed. Transcribing-machine operators may also have various clerical duties, such as answering the telephones and filing correspondence.

■ *Technical stenographers* may specialize in medical, legal, engineering, or other technical areas. They should be familiar with the terminology and the practice of the appropriate subject. For example, a *medical transcriptionist* must be a medical language expert and be familiar with the processes of patient assessment, therapeutic procedures, diagnoses, and prognoses. (See the article "Medical Transcriptionists" for more information.)

■ *Court reporters* specialize in taking notes for and transcribing legal and court proceedings.

■ *Real-time captioners* operate CAT stenotype systems to create English closed captions for live television broadcasts.

Note that the body of knowledge required to perform the tasks of a court reporter or real-time captioner is greater than that which a stenographer needs to know. While a court reporter or captioner could readily perform the tasks of an office stenographer, the stenographer would be unable to perform either job without additional training.

REQUIREMENTS

High School
Although there are no specific educational requirements for this type of career, most stenographers should have a high school diploma. Some high school students follow a business education curriculum and take courses in typing, shorthand, and business procedures. These students may later enter a business school or college for more advanced technical training. Other students may follow a general education program and take courses in English, history, mathematics, and the sciences, intending to undergo all of their technical training after graduation.

Postsecondary Training
Although some students with a business curriculum background are able to obtain jobs immediately after graduation from high school, better job opportunities and higher salaries may be more readily available to those who have sought advanced technical training, a col-

History of the Stenograph

1879: Miles M. Bartholomew invents first successful American short-hand machine.

1930s: While working for the LaSalle Stenotype Company, Milton "M. H." Wright uses the Master Model Stenotype and realizes its shortcomings. Wright's son, Robert, works on improvements to the machine. Robert refines the machine and is awarded patents for the new, improved machine, called the Stenograph.

1938: Wright resigns from LaSalle and starts Stenograph Corporation, which was originally known as Stenographic Machines. The business is incorporated in May in the state of Illinois. Two new models of the Stenograph machine are offered, the Secretarial and the Court Reporter.

1946: After the company survives the wartime shortage of materials, business for Stenograph booms.

1948: Robert Wright joins the Stenograph Company and begins to implement more changes to improve the machines.

1949: Trademark for the Stenograph name is officially signed.

1950: Adjustable key-length and tension features are introduced.

1960s: The Stenograph is used to assist in the development of a computerized language translation system.

1964: Stenograph partners with IBM to develop the first computer-aided transcription (CAT) system.

1978: Stenograph introduces CAT to the court reporting industry.

1996: Stenograph is purchased by The Heico Companies, which provides financial strength and a better market position for the company.

lege degree, or some avenue of specialization. In many instances, training at a business school, vocational school, or college may be required. Those considering the more advanced career of court reporter or real-time captioner should earn at least a two-year degree in court and conference reporting, although a four-year degree that includes courses in computers and English is preferable.

Numerous opportunities for advanced training exist. Hundreds of business schools and colleges throughout the country offer technical or degree programs with both day and evening classes. These schools can be located in the telephone directory or by contacting individual state employment services.

Certification or Licensing

Some stenographers, especially those who work for the federal government, may belong to a union such as the Office and Professional Employees' International Union. To work for the federal government, stenographers must pass a civil service test and be able to take dictation at the rate of 80 words per minute and type at least 40 words per minute. Tests of verbal and mathematical ability are also required. Employers in the private sector may require similar tests. Certification is available for advanced jobs, such as court reporters, real-time captioners, and medical transcriptionists.

Other Requirements

Stenographers should have good reading comprehension and spelling skills, as well as good finger and hand dexterity. They should also find systematic and orderly work appealing, and they should like to work on detailed tasks. Other personal qualifications include dependability, trustworthiness, and a neat personal appearance, given their high degree of visibility.

EXPLORING

You can get experience in the stenography field by assuming clerical and typing responsibilities with a school club or other organization. In addition, some school work-study programs may have opportunities with businesses for part-time, on-the-job training. It may also be possible to get a part-time or summer job in a business office by contacting offices on your own. You may have the opportunity to get training in the operation of word processors and other office machinery through evening or continuing education courses offered by business schools and community colleges.

EMPLOYERS

Stenographers, including those who have developed special skills through training, are employed in various organizations of law, business, and federal, state, and local government. Some specialist stenographers work in medical, legal, engineering, or other technical areas. Some stenographers develop their own freelance businesses.

STARTING OUT

High school guidance counselors and business education teachers may be helpful in locating job opportunities for would-be stenographers. Additionally, business schools and colleges frequently have placement programs to help their trainees and graduates find employment. Those interested in securing an entry-level position can also contact individual businesses or government agencies directly. Jobs may also be located through newspaper classified ads.

Many companies administer aptitude tests to potential employees before they are hired. Speed and accuracy are critical factors in making such evaluations. Individuals who are initially unable to meet the minimum requirements for a stenographer position may want to take jobs as typists or clerks and, as they gain experience and technical training, try for promotion to the position of stenographer.

ADVANCEMENT

Skilled stenographers can advance to secretarial positions, especially if they develop their interpersonal communications skills. They may also become heads of stenographic departments or in some cases be promoted to office manager. In some instances, experienced stenographers may go into business for themselves as public stenographers serving traveling business people and others. Stenographers who complete advanced training may become court reporters, real-time captioners, or medical transcriptionists.

EARNINGS

Salaries for stenographers vary widely, depending on their skill, experience, level of responsibility, and geographic location. New workers may earn as little $14,000 a year, while the most experienced stenographers may earn $33,000 or more annually. Full-time workers also receive paid vacation, health insurance, and other benefits.

WORK ENVIRONMENT

Relatively few office stenographers work in the evenings or on weekends. (This is not true of court reporters, real-time captioners, or those who freelance their services, as they often work long and irregular hours.) Some stenographers take on part-time or temporary work during peak business periods.

The physical work environment is usually pleasant and comfortable, although stenographers may sometimes have to work under extreme deadline pressure. Stenographers may also be subject to repetitive stress injury, a prevalent industrial hazard for those who perform repeated motions in their daily work. Carpal tunnel syndrome is a type of repetitive stress injury that stenographers can sometimes develop, causing a prickling sensation or numbness in the hand and sometimes a partial loss of function. Stenographers generally perform their jobs while seated and so must be conscious of correct posture and proper seating.

The majority of stenographers are not required to travel; however, some may accompany their employers on business trips to provide dictation services.

OUTLOOK

Job opportunities for unspecialized stenographers have been declining and should continue to fall off sharply in the coming years. Audio recording equipment and the use of personal computers by managers and other professionals has greatly reduced the demand for these workers, while increasing demand for CAT system operators in real-time settings. The trend to provide instantaneous captions for the deaf and hearing-impaired and the growing use of CAT technology in courtroom trials should strengthen the demand for real-time reporters. Continued technological advances, such as computer-aided equipment that can print out what is being said by a spoken voice, will imperil this profession further.

Despite this decline, however, some jobs will become available as people retire or otherwise leave the profession. As always, those with the most skill and experience, or a particular area of expertise (such as legal or medical stenographers) will have the best employment possibilities.

FOR MORE INFORMATION

For information on union membership, contact:
Office and Professional Employees International Union
265 West 14th Street, 6th Floor
New York, NY 10011
Tel: 800-346-7348
Email: opeiu@opeiu.org
http://www.opeiu.org

Stock Clerks

OVERVIEW

Stock clerks receive, unpack, store, distribute, and record the inventory for materials or products used by a company, plant, or store. Approximately 1.68 million stock clerks are employed in the United States.

HISTORY

Almost every type of business establishment imaginable—shoe store, restaurant, hotel, auto repair shop, hospital, supermarket, or steel mill—buys materials or products from outside distributors and uses these materials in its operations. A large part of the company's money is tied up in these inventory stocks, but without them operations would come to a standstill. Stores would run out of merchandise to sell, mechanics would be unable to repair cars until new parts were shipped in, and factories would be unable to operate once their basic supply of raw materials ran out.

To avoid these problems, businesses have developed their own inventory-control systems to store enough goods and raw materials for uninterrupted operations, move these materials to the places they are needed, and know when it is time to order more. These systems are the responsibility of stock clerks.

QUICK FACTS

School Subjects
English
Mathematics

Personal Skills
Following instructions

Work Environment
Primarily indoors
Primarily one location

Minimum Education Level
High school diploma

Salary Range
$10,712 to $19,060 to
$35,230+

Certification or Licensing
None available

Outlook
Little change or more slowly
than the average

DOT
222

GOE
05.09.01

NOC
1474

O*NET-SOC
43-5081.00, 43-5081.01,
43-5081.02, 43-5081.03,
43-5081.04

THE JOB

Stock clerks work in just about every type of industry, and no matter what kind of storage or stock room they staff—food, clothing, merchandise, medicine, or raw materials—the work of stock clerks is essentially the same. They receive, sort, put away, distribute, and keep track of the items a business sells or uses. Their titles sometimes vary based on their responsibilities.

When goods are received in a stockroom, stock clerks unpack the shipment and check the contents against documents such as the invoice, purchase order, and bill of lading, which lists the contents of the shipment. The shipment is inspected, and any damaged goods are set aside. Stock clerks may reject or send back damaged items or call vendors to complain about the condition of the shipment. In large companies this work may be done by a shipping and receiving clerk.

Once the goods are received, stock clerks organize them and sometimes mark them with identifying codes or prices so they can be placed in stock according to the existing inventory system. In this way the materials or goods can be found readily when needed, and inventory control is much easier. In many firms stock clerks use hand-held scanners and computers to keep inventory records up to date.

In retail stores and supermarkets, stock clerks may bring merchandise to the sales floor and stock shelves and racks. In stockrooms and warehouses they store materials in bins, on the floor, or on shelves. In other settings, such as restaurants, hotels, and factories, stock clerks deliver goods when they are needed. They may do this on a regular schedule or at the request of other employees or supervisors. Although many stock clerks use mechanical equipment, such as forklifts, to move heavy items, some perform strenuous and laborious work. In general, the work of a stock clerk involves much standing, bending, walking, stretching, lifting, and carrying.

When items are removed from the inventory, stock clerks adjust records to reflect the products' use. These records are kept as current as possible, and inventories are periodically checked against these records. Every item is counted, and the totals are compared with the records on hand or the records from the sales, shipping, production, or purchasing departments. This helps identify how fast items are being used, when items must be ordered from outside suppliers, or even whether items are disappearing from the stockroom. Many retail establishments use computerized cash registers that maintain an inventory count automatically as they record the sale of each item.

The duties of stock clerks vary depending on their place of employment. Stock clerks working in small firms perform many different tasks, including shipping and receiving, inventory control, and purchasing. In large firms, responsibilities may be more narrowly defined. More specific job categories include inventory clerks, stock control clerks, material clerks, order fillers, merchandise distributors, and shipping and receiving clerks.

At a construction site or factory that uses a variety of raw and finished materials, there are many different types of specialized work for

A stock clerk checks the inventory on a supermarket shelf. *(Corbis)*

stock clerks. *Tool crib attendants* issue, receive, and store the various hand tools, machine tools, dies, and other equipment used in an industrial establishment. They make sure the tools come back in reasonably good shape and keep track of those that need replacing. *Parts order and stock clerks* purchase, store, and distribute the spare parts needed for motor vehicles and other industrial equipment. *Metal control coordinators* oversee the movement of metal stock and supplies used in producing nonferrous metal sheets, bars, tubing, and alloys. In mining and other industries that regularly use explosives, *magazine keepers* store explosive materials and components safely and distribute them to authorized personnel. In the military, *space and storage clerks* keep track of the weights and amounts of ammunition and explosive components stored in the magazines of an arsenal and check their storage condition.

Many types of stock clerks can be found in other industries. At printing companies, *cut-file clerks* collect, store, and hand out the layout cuts, ads, mats, and electrotypes used in the printing process. *Parts clerks* handle and distribute spare and replacement parts in repair and maintenance shops. In eyeglass centers, *prescription clerks* select the lens blanks and frames for making eyeglasses and keep inventory stocked at a specified level. In motion picture companies, *property custodians* receive, store, and distribute the props needed for shooting. In hotels and hospitals, *linen room attendants* issue and keep track of inventories of bed linen, tablecloths, and uniforms, while *kitchen clerks* verify the quantity and quality of food products being taken from the storeroom to the kitchen. Aboard ships, the clerk in charge of receiving and issuing supplies and keeping track of inventory is known as the *storekeeper*.

REQUIREMENTS

High School

Although there are no specific educational requirements for beginning stock clerks, employers prefer to hire high school graduates. Reading and writing skills and a basic knowledge of mathematics are necessary; typing and filing skills are also useful. In the future, as more companies install computerized inventory systems, a knowledge of computer operations will be important.

Other Requirements

Good health and good eyesight is important. A willingness to take orders from supervisors and others is necessary for this work, as is the ability to follow directions. Organizational skills also are important, as is neatness. Depending on where you work, you may be required to join a union. This is especially true of stock clerks who are employed by industry and who work in large cities with a high percentage of union-affiliated companies.

When a stock clerk handles certain types of materials, extra training or certification may be required. Generally those who handle jewelry, liquor, or drugs must be bonded.

EXPLORING

The best way to learn about the responsibilities of a stock clerk is to get a part-time or summer job as a sales clerk, stockroom helper, stockroom clerk, or, in some factories, stock chaser. These jobs are relatively easy to get and can help you learn about stock work, as well as about the duties of workers in related positions. This sort of part-time work can also lead to a full-time job.

EMPLOYERS

About 1.68 million people work as stock clerks. Almost 76 percent of stock clerks work in retail and wholesale firms, and the remainder work in hospitals, factories, government agencies, schools, and other organizations. Nearly all sales floor stock clerks are employed in retail establishments, with about two-thirds working in supermarkets.

STARTING OUT

Job openings for stock clerks often are listed in newspaper classified ads. Job seekers should contact the personnel office of the firm looking for stock clerks and fill out an application for employment. School counselors, parents, relatives, and friends also can be good sources for job leads and may be able to give personal references if an employer requires them.

Stock clerks usually receive on-the-job training. New workers start with simple tasks, such as counting and marking stock. The basic responsibilities of the job are usually learned within the first few weeks. As they progress, stock clerks learn to keep records of incoming and outgoing materials, take inventories, and place orders. As wholesale and warehousing establishments convert to automated inventory systems, stock clerks need to be trained to use the new equipment. Stock clerks who bring merchandise to the sales floor and stock shelves and sales racks need little training.

ADVANCEMENT

Stock clerks with ability and determination have a good chance of being promoted to jobs with greater responsibility. In small firms, stock clerks may advance to sales positions or become assistant buyers or purchasing agents. In large firms, stock clerks can advance to more responsible stock-handling jobs, such as invoice clerk, stock control clerk, and procurement clerk.

Furthering one's education can lead to more opportunities for advancement. By studying at a technical or business school or taking home-study courses, stock clerks can prove to their employer that they have the intelligence and ambition to take on more important tasks. More advanced positions, such as warehouse manager and purchasing agent, are usually given to experienced people who have post-high school education.

EARNINGS

Beginning stock clerks usually earn the minimum wage or slightly more. The U.S. Department of Labor reports that stock clerks earned a median annual salary of $19,060 in 2001. Experienced stock clerks can earn anywhere from $13,260 to more than $35,230, with time-and-a-half pay for overtime. Average earnings vary depending on the type of industry and geographic location. Stock clerks working in the retail trade generally earn wages in the middle range. In transportation, utilities, and wholesale businesses, earnings usually are higher; in finance, insurance, real estate, and other types of office services, earnings generally are lower. Those working for large companies or national chains may receive excellent benefits. After one year of employment, some stock clerks are offered one to two weeks of paid vacation each year, as well as health and medical insurance and a retirement plan.

WORK ENVIRONMENT

Stock clerks usually work in relatively clean, comfortable areas. Working conditions vary considerably, however, depending on the industry and type of merchandise being handled. For example, stock clerks who handle refrigerated goods must spend some time in cold storage rooms, while those who handle construction materials, such as bricks and lumber, occasionally work outside in harsh weather. Most stock clerk jobs involve much standing, bending, walking, stretching, lifting, and carrying. Some workers may be required to operate machinery to lift and move stock.

Because stock clerks are employed in so many different types of industries, the amount of hours worked every week depends on the type of employer. Stock clerks in retail stores usually work a five-day, 40-hour week, while those in industry work 44 hours, or five and one-half days, a week. Many others are able to find part-time work. Overtime is common, especially when large shipments arrive or during peak times such as holiday seasons.

OUTLOOK

Although the volume of inventory transactions is expected to increase significantly, employment for stock clerks is expected to grow more slowly than the average for all occupations over the next several years, according to the U.S. Department of Labor. This is a result of increased automation and other productivity improvements that enable clerks to handle more stock. Manufacturing and wholesale trade industries are making the greatest use of automation. In addition to computerized inventory control systems, firms in these industries are expected to rely more on sophisticated conveyor belts, automatic high stackers to store and retrieve goods, and automatic guided vehicles that are battery-powered and driverless. Sales floor stock clerks probably will be less affected by automation as most of their work is done on the sales floor, where it is difficult to locate or operate complicated machinery.

Because this occupation employs a large number of workers, many job openings will occur each year to replace stock clerks who transfer to other jobs and leave the labor force. Stock clerk jobs tend to be entry-level positions, so many vacancies will be created by normal career progression to other occupations.

FOR MORE INFORMATION

For materials on educational programs in the retail industry, contact:
National Retail Federation
325 7th Street, NW, Suite 1100
Washington, DC 20004
http://www.nrf.com

Typists and Word Processors

QUICK FACTS

School Subjects
Computer science
English

Personal Skills
Following instructions
Mechanical/manipulative

Work Environment
Primarily indoors
Primarily one location

Minimum Education Level
High school diploma

Salary Range
$15,640 to $26,000 to
$38,260+

Certification or Licensing
None available

Outlook
Decline

DOT
203

GOE
07.06.02

NOC
1411

O*NET-SOC
43-9021, 43-9022.00

OVERVIEW

Using typewriters, personal computers, and other office machines, *typists* and *word processors* convert handwritten or otherwise unfinished material into clean, readable, typewritten copies. Typists create reports, letters, forms, tables, charts, and other materials for all kinds of businesses and services. Word processors create the same types of materials using a computer that stores information electronically instead of printing it directly onto paper. Other typists use special machines that convert manuscripts into Braille, coded copy, or typeset copy. Typists, word processors, and data entry keyers hold about 634,000 jobs in the United States.

HISTORY

The invention of the typewriter in 1829 by W. A. Burt greatly increased business efficiency and productivity, and its benefits increased as typists became skilled at quickly transforming messy handwritten documents into neat, consistently typed copies.

More recently, the introduction of word processing into the workplace has revolutionized typing. This task may be done on a personal computer, a computer terminal hooked up to a network, or a computer that strictly handles word processing functions. As a person types, the words appear on a video display terminal screen. Workers can correct errors and make any necessary changes right on the screen before a hard copy is printed on paper, thus eliminating the need for retyping whole pages to correct mistakes. The computer stores the information in its memory, so the worker can go back to it again and again for copies or changes.

The term "word processing" entered the English language in 1965, when International Business Machines, more commonly known as IBM, introduced a typewriter that put information onto magnetic tape instead of paper. Corrections could be made on this tape before running the tape through a machine that converted the signals on the tape into characters on a printed page. Today, word processing software and personal computers have virtually replaced typewriters in the office.

THE JOB

Some typists perform few duties other than typing. These workers spend approximately 75 percent of their time at the keyboard. They may input statistical data, medical reports, legal briefs, addresses, letters, and other documents from handwritten copies. They may work in pools, dividing the work of a large office among many workers under the supervision of a typing section chief. These typists may also be responsible for making photocopies of typewritten materials for distribution.

Beginning typists may start by typing address labels, headings on form letters, and documents from legible handwritten copy. More experienced typists may work from copy that is more difficult to read or needs to be printed in tabular form.

Clerk-typists spend up to 50 percent of their time typing. They also perform a variety of clerical tasks such as filing, answering the phone, acting as receptionists, and operating copy machines.

Many typists type from recorded audio tapes instead of written or printed copy. *Transcribing-machine operators* sit at keyboards and wear headsets, through which they hear the spoken contents of letters, reports, and meetings. Typists can control the speed of the tape so they can comfortably type every word they hear. They proofread their finished documents and may erase dictated tapes for future reuse.

Many typists work at computer terminals. *Magnetic-tape typewriter operators* enter information from written materials on computers to produce magnetic disks or tapes for storage and later retrieval. *In-file operators* use terminals to post or receive information about people's credit records for credit reporting agencies. When an agency subscriber calls with a question about a person's credit, the typist calls up that record on the video display terminal screen and reads the information.

Most common of the computer typists are *word processors.* These employees put documents into the proper format by entering codes into the word processing software, telling it which lines to center, which words to underline, where the margins should be set, and so forth, and how the document should be stored and printed. Word processors can edit, change, insert, and delete materials instantly by just by pressing keys. Word processing is particularly efficient for form letters, in which only certain parts of a document change on each copy. When a word processor has finished formatting and keying in a document, it is electronically sent to a printer for a finished copy. The document is normally saved on a disk or the computer's hard drive so that any subsequent changes to it can be made easily and new copies produced immediately. Word processors also can send electronic files via email or modems to people in different locations.

Certain typists use special machines to create copy. *Perforator typists* type on machines that punch holes in a paper tape, which is used to create typewritten copy automatically. In publishing and printing, *photocomposing-perforator machine operators, photocomposing-keyboard operators, veritype operators,* and *typesetter-perforator operators* type on special machines that produce photographic negatives or paper prints of the copy. Some of these typists must also code copy to show what size and style of letters and characters should be used and how the layout of the page should look.

Braille typists and *Braille operators* use special typewriter-like machines to transcribe written or spoken English into Braille. By pressing one key or a combination of keys, they create the raised characters of the Braille alphabet. They may print either on special paper or on metal plates, which are later used to print books or other publications.

Cryptographic machine operators operate typewriter-like equipment that codes, transmits, and decodes secret messages for the armed forces, law enforcement agencies, and business organizations. These typists select a code card from a code book, insert the card into the machine, and type the message in English on the machine, which converts it to coded copy. A decoding card is used to follow the same process for decoding.

REQUIREMENTS

High School

Most employers require that typists and word processors be high school graduates and able to type accurately at a rate of at least 40 or 50 words per minute. Typists need a good knowledge of spelling, grammar, and punctuation and may be required to be familiar with standard office equipment.

Postsecondary Training

In addition to high schools, there are colleges, business schools, and home-study courses that teach keyboarding skills. Some people learn keyboarding through self-teaching materials such as books, recordings, and computer programs. Business schools and community colleges often offer certificates or associate's degrees for typists and word processors.

For those who do not pursue such formal education, temporary agencies will often train workers in these skills. Generally, it takes a minimum of three to six months of experience to become a skilled word processor.

Word processors must be able to type 45–80 words per minute and should know the proper way to organize such documents as letters, reports, and financial statements. Increasingly, employers are requiring that employees know how to use various software programs for word processing, spreadsheet, and database management tasks.

Other Requirements

To be a successful typist and word processor, you need manual dexterity and the ability to concentrate. You should be alert, efficient, and attentive to detail. Because you will often work directly with other people, you need good interpersonal skills, including a courteous and cheerful demeanor. Good listening skills are important in order to transcribe recorded material.

EXPLORING

As with many clerical occupations, a good way to gain experience as a typist is through high school work-study programs. Students in these programs work part-time for local businesses and attend classes part-time. Temporary agencies also provide training and temporary jobs for exploring the field. Another way to gain typing experience is to volunteer to type for friends, church groups, or other organizations and to create your own computerized reports.

EMPLOYERS

Typists and word processors are employed in almost every kind of workplace, including banks, law firms, factories, schools, hospitals, publishing firms, department stores, and government agencies. They may work with groups of employees in large offices or with only one or two other people in small offices.

Of the 634,000 data entry and information processing workers, approximately 405,000 are data entry keyers and 229,000 are word processors and typists. About one-third of all data entry and information processing workers work in firms that provide business services, including temporary help, word processing, and computer and data processing. Nearly one out of five work in federal, state, and local government agencies.

STARTING OUT

Business school and college students may learn of typing or word processing positions through their schools' placement offices. Some large businesses recruit employees directly from these schools. High school guidance counselors also may know of local job openings.

People interested in typing or word processor positions can check the want ads in newspapers and business journals for companies with job openings. They can apply directly to the personnel departments of large companies that hire many of these workers. They also can register with temporary agencies. To apply for positions with the federal government, job seekers should apply at the nearest regional Office of Personnel Management. State, county, and city governments may also have listings for such positions.

ADVANCEMENT

Typists and word processors usually receive salary increases as they gain experience and are promoted from junior to senior positions. These are often given a classification or pay scale designation, such as typist or word processor I or II. They may also advance from clerk-typist to technical typist, or from a job in a typing pool to a typing position in a private office.

A degree in business management or executive secretarial skills increases a typist's chances for advancement. In addition, many large companies and government agencies provide training programs that allow workers to upgrade their skills and move into other jobs, such as secretary, statistical clerk, or stenographer.

Once they have acquired enough experience, some typists and word processors go into business for themselves and provide typing services to business clients working from their homes. They may find work typing reports, manuscripts, and papers for professors, authors, business people, and students.

The more word processing experience an employee has, the better the opportunities to move up. Some may be promoted to word processing supervisor or selected for in-house professional training programs in data processing. Word processors may also move into related fields and work as word-processing equipment salespeople or servicers, or word-processing teachers or consultants.

EARNINGS

The U.S. Department of Labor reports that median annual earnings of word processors and typists in 2001 were $26,000. Salaries ranged from less than $17,100 to more than $38,260. Median annual earnings of data entry keyers in 2001 were $21,960, and salaries ranged from less than $15,640 to more than $31,270. The average annual salary for all clerk-typists in the federal government was $24,934 in 2001.

Typists and word processors occasionally may work overtime to finish special projects and may receive overtime pay. In large cities workers usually receive paid holidays, two weeks' vacation after one year of employment, sick leave, health and life insurance, and a pension plan. Some large companies also provide dental insurance, profit sharing opportunities, and bonuses.

WORK ENVIRONMENT

Typists and word processors usually work 35–40 hours per week at work stations in clean, bright offices. They usually sit most of the day in a fairly small area. The work is detailed and often repetitious, and approaching deadlines may increase the pressure and demands placed on typists and word processors.

Recent years have seen a controversy develop concerning the effect that working at video display terminals (VDTs) can have on workers' health. Working with these screens in improper lighting can cause eyestrain, and sitting at a workstation all day can cause musculoskeletal stress and pain. The computer industry is paying closer attention to these problems and is working to improve health and safety standards in VDT-equipped offices.

Another common ailment for typists and word processors is carpal tunnel syndrome, a painful ailment of the tendons in the wrist that is triggered by repetitive movement. If left unchecked, it can require corrective surgery. However, proper placement of the typing keyboard can help prevent injury. Several companies have designed desks, chairs, and working spaces that accommodate the physical needs of typists and word processors in the best manner currently known.

The nature of this work lends itself to flexible work arrangements. Many typists and word processors work in temporary positions that provide flexible schedules. About 20 percent work part time. Some offices allow word processors and typists to telecommute from home, whereby they receive and send work on home computers via modems. These jobs may be especially convenient for workers with disabilities or family responsibilities, but often they do not provide a full range of benefits and lack the advantages of social interaction on the job.

OUTLOOK

Employment in the typing field is expected to decline over the next several years due to the increasing automation of offices. However, the sheer size of the occupation means that many jobs will become available for typists and word processors, especially to replace those employees who change careers or leave the workforce.

Technological innovations such as scanners, voice-recognition software, and electronic data transmission are being used in more workplaces, reducing the need for typists and word processors. Many office workers now do their own word processing because word processing and data entry software has become so user-friendly.

More companies today are contracting out their data entry and word processing projects to temporary-help and staffing services firms. Most openings will be with these types of firms, and jobs will go to workers who have the best technical skills and knowledge of several word processing programs.

FOR MORE INFORMATION

For membership information, contact:
Association of Business Support Services International
5852 Oak Meadow Drive
Yorba Linda, CA 92886-5930
Tel: 714-695-9398
Email: info@abssi.org
http://www.abssi.org

For industry information, contact the IAAP:
International Association of Administrative Professionals (IAAP)
10502 NW Ambassador Drive
PO Box 20404
Kansas City, MO 64195-0404
Tel: 816-891-6600
Email: service@iaap-hq.org
http://www.iaap-hq.org

INTERVIEW

Elizabeth Sakanis works from home as a typist and word processor for several companies in the Chicagoland area. She spoke to the editors of Careers in Focus: Clerks & Administrative Workers *about her career.*

Q. Please briefly describe your primary and secondary job duties.

A. As a typist, my primary duty is to type the project as accurately and timely as possible. The secondary duty is to make sure the project is delivered per the customer's instructions.

Q. How did you train to become a typist?

A. I took typing and office machine classes throughout high school. That was the only formal training I had.

Q. How/where did you get your first job in this field? What did you do?

A. My first job was at Harris Bank in downtown Chicago in 1978. I was hired into the word processing unit as a statistical typist on a typewriter. When the unit totally went to computers, I became a word processor. I worked my way through the ranks in the unit and when they opened a word processing satellite office in another building, I was in charge of that unit until I left the company.

Q. What kind of sources were and are available to someone looking to get into this field? Newspaper classifieds? Word of mouth? Job search agencies? Internet?

A. Back when I started, I went to an employment agency to find the job. At the time it didn't seem like word of mouth or newspaper classifieds were bountiful. Now you can look in classifieds, employment agencies, or on the Internet.

Q. What are the most important personal and professional qualities for typists?

A. The kind of typing job you get will affect the personal and professional qualities you need. When I worked at the bank I had to deal with customers on a day-to-day basis. I also had to answer the phone and talk to customers, so I needed both a good personality and I needed to be very professional with the customers. I've been doing typing out of my home for approximately six years now. While I'm in a relaxed atmosphere at home, I still need to be professional and have a good personality when dealing with customers.

Q. What are some of the pros and cons of your job?

A. The biggest pro of typing out of my house is that I can make my own hours and still be here for my family. The biggest con of typing nowadays is that you don't see a lot of ads or need for just typists any more. They have to have a little more than typing skills to back them up.

Q. What is the most important piece of advice that you have to offer people interested in working in this field?

A. My advice for anyone who likes to type is to get some other training. For instance, go into desktop publishing or become a medical transcriptionist or work in a related field. There's not a lot of demand for just a typist any more, but I see more and more ads for desktop publishing and transcription.

Index